CULTURE & CUSTOMISATION

Published in October 2021

ISBN 978-1-910505-74-8

Published by Evro Publishing, Westrow House, Holwell, Sherborne, Dorset DT9 5LF, UK

Printed and bound in Slovenia by DZS Grafik

Illustrated, written and designed by Barry John

The Author

Like every boy in the 1950s, Barry John knew the names of John Cobb and Malcolm Campbell and possessed battered Dinky toys of their cars. His fascination with record-breaking has persisted to this day and led to his first book, *Quest for Speed* (Evro, 2020), which he wrote, illustrated and designed himself. Riding various scooters in the 1960s sparked another lifelong interest and now he has applied his professional skills — he studied at Harrow School of Art and worked as a graphic designer — to his love of scooter culture.

THE MOTOR SCOOTER STORY

BARRY JOHN

EVRO
PUBLISHING

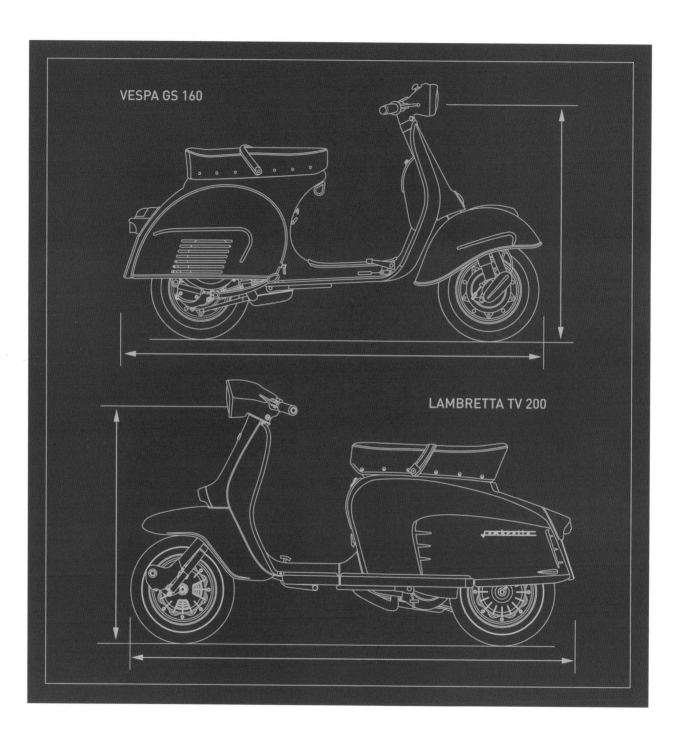

VESPA GS 160

LAMBRETTA TV 200

CONTENTS

*"I gave my future wife a lift on my
scooter, the rest is history."*

*"The scooters, clothes and music
— an unforgettable time of my life."*

*"Exciting, fun and carefree days when
anything seemed possible."*

INTRODUCTION

The subject of this story has often been referred to as the 'humble' motor scooter. Things, however, are not always what they seem. The scooter developed from the very beginning into a joyous form of transport that eventually captivated the world. The Italians were far from being the first to create the motor scooter. Its history stretches all the way back to 1915 in America and the design slowly evolved from there. The earliest mass-produced stand-on type may have been regarded as a novelty mode of transport for middle-class working women who could afford such a luxury yet was functional enough to be adopted by New York traffic cops.

In 1920 something similar appeared in Britain but with the sensible addition of a seat. Another British machine arrived that year to predate the design of later scooters with legshields, a step-through footboard and fluid body lines. Unfortunately, although ahead of its time, this vehicle was too expensive at almost £100 (half the price of a cheap car) and disappeared in 1922.

Back across the Atlantic the Americans were working on their own ideas. In 1935 a scooter with an automatic gearbox came on the market. This continuously variable transmission was a sign of things to come. It is in common use today for scooters throughout the world. These single-seat American scooters were still at an embryonic stage. Their small wheels and low performance did not encourage confidence for holding one's own on busy roads inhabited by large automobiles and trucks. They were more suitable for delivering newspapers from the pavement and were seen whizzing actors around private film lots in Hollywood. The second generation of American scooters in the 1940s were bigger, quite rugged and more powerful. With some storage space they were a viable proposition for delivery companies and other small business users. Claims of 75 miles or more to the gallon made the cost of running them attractively economical with gasoline costing less than 20 cents per gallon.

The onset of the Second World War might have brought production to a halt if the American military had not found a use for this particular vehicle.

By doing so a creative process was put into motion that would have an effect far beyond the borders of the United States. The cessation of domestic vehicle production worldwide during the conflict caused a vacuum in the post-war years. This was exploited by the Italians, who led the way, and the scooter paradigm was further tightened up with enclosed transmission systems, handlebar controls, dual seats, a small-capacity two-stroke engine and tyres standardised at about 16 inches diameter. A wider market was found by putting the machines into a cultural, as well as purely functional, context. Many other manufacturers followed. Punching above its weight and lending itself to a wide range of applications, the motor scooter was soon produced all over the world — helping to regenerate many economies. In the UK during one unique period, scooters flowered in a kaleidoscope of colour and individuality, such that it was rare to see two quite the same. In impoverished countries, scooters allowed people to get around on dusty roads where there was no public transport. This never-ending story continues today.

AN IDEA RISES FROM THE RUBBLE

When Benito Mussolini, in his wisdom, signed the Tripartite Pact with Germany and Japan on 27 September 1940 he sealed the fate of his country. The ill-trained and poorly equipped Italian army had no real heart for the conflict and surrendered by the tens of thousands in North Africa. In the meantime the RAF and later the USAAF applied strategic bombing

to industrial centres in the north of Italy and the railway network. Sicily was then invaded, beginning on 9 July 1943 with a paratroop drop by the American 82nd Airborne. The invasion of Italy followed, beginning on 3 September, and the 82nd Airborne were deployed on the Italian mainland. Battered into submission, a demoralised Italy surrendered to the Allies soon after but the Germans occupied much of the country to resist the allied armies, and the destruction continued. Rural dirt roads were mashed to oblivion by convoys of trucks and armoured vehicles. City roads fared little better and train systems were annihilated.

Enrico Piaggio and Ferdinando Innocenti both witnessed the bombs that rained from the sky to obliterate their respective industrial plants in Pontedera and Milan. When Italy switched allegiance to the Allied side the two men began to think of ways to salvage something from the disastrous consequences of Mussolini's bombastic ambitions. Ironically the inspirational seeds for the green shoots of their recovery also descended from above.

As ground troops, the 82nd Airborne were supplied with the Cushman Model 32 scooter for communication purposes between their units and when they pounded their way up the boot of Italy these agile machines went with them. By the time Rome was liberated on 4 June 1944 the 82nd had been issued with the Cushman Model 53, a lightened version of their scooter that could be dropped in crates by parachute. The British paras also had a presence in Italy and used the Excelsior Welbike, which was also air-dropped in canisters.

With the war still raging in the north, Enrico Piaggio and Ferdinando Innocenti observed these practical machines whizzing around the battered streets of Rome. Both these previously wealthy industrialists needed to find a way to revitalise their factories by diversifying into something other than war material.

Benito's grandiose delusions led to his own assassination and left his country on its knees. Italy's economy was in cardiac arrest, its life-support

CUSHMAN MODEL 32

CUSHMAN MODEL 53

currency consisted of American Hershey bars and cigarettes. Industrial output was at a standstill. Railways were paralysed, the roads pulverised and petrol rationed. With many Italians unemployed and at starvation level, it was a long way back. One of the priorities was to get the country and the economy moving again. Both Piaggio and Innocenti saw the light.

The Cushman military scooters had sparked their vision of the future. Even while the rubble of their factories still lay behind enemy lines, they both began design work on prototypes based on the Cushman step-through design, which was a departure from conventional motorcycle practice. Motive power was also to be different. Unlike the 4.6 horsepower four-stroke Cushmans, the British Welbike, which was more like a pocket-sized motorcycle, was powered by a smaller, less complicated Villiers two-stroke engine. This idea was also adopted by the Italian entrepreneurs as it was cheaper to manufacture.

The basic ingredients of the modern scooter were beginning to come together and the two men entered a period of intense competition.

PIAGGIO FIRST TO THE POTHOLES

The Piaggio company was founded in 1894 to produce railway carriages. In the 1920s it diversified into aircraft production, went on to set many world records and began supplying the Italian Air Force with modern planes. By the time Italy had surrendered to the Allies, the bottom had fallen out of the four-engine Italian bomber market. The Germans had shipped much of the valuable machinery back to their homeland and mined the buildings. Allied strategic bombing finished the job, leaving what machinery remained to rust unprotected. Knowing that aircraft production was now restricted by the Allies and even automobile

THE PAPERINO

1946 VESPA 90

manufacture would be out of the question, Enrico Piaggio embarked on his epic scooter adventure. This began not with a bang but a quack. Enter the Paperino — translated as Donald Duck. As Piaggio disliked this first prototype with its high footwell and clumsy lines, he turned to aeronautic designer Corradino D'Ascanio, who had been commissioned by Innocenti but fallen out with him, for a new approach.

D'Ascanio's previous background in aeronautics was reflected in the design. He did not like motorcycles so devised a new concept inspired by the Cushman but taken to a new level. The machine was based on a pressed-steel spar frame, a structure that today would be termed a semi-monocoque. Traditionally vehicles were based on a chassis with everything bolted to it. This was a very different idea more in line with aircraft design wherein the bodywork was the chassis. In place of traditional front forks there was a single arm, similar to an aircraft's landing gear, that made tyre changing much easier. The usual oily exposed chain drive was eliminated by making the 98cc engine, gearbox and rear wheel

drive integral with the system enclosed. The hot exhaust system was tucked away. Putting the gear lever on the handlebars and providing adequate leg shields together with the step-through design made it easier and cleaner for both men and women to get on the

machine and drive. When this second prototype, known as the MP 6, was shown to Enrico Piaggio, he exclaimed that it looked like a wasp and so, without realising it, named the creation. Wasp in Italian is *vespa*. By such turns

of fate the Vespa was born.

Piaggio himself was sold on the little machine and his faith in it was strong enough to go into production without any orders up front. With help from the Allies, Piaggio's stolen machinery was retrieved and some parts of the Pontedera factory were rebuilt. In April 1946, with nerves of steel, he began a 2,500 production run of a slightly refined version of the prototype and named it the Vespa 98. With a speed of 37mph and 118mpg, his vision of a stylish machine for the masses was an immediate success. Although less than ten per cent of Italian households had both electricity and running water, the Vespa became a must-have item.

Output rose to 10,535 in 1947 and 19,822 in 1948. Demand was now strong enough to produce Vespas under licence in Germany, a move that pushed total production to 60,000 by 1950. Piaggio kept this success going by reinvesting in a racing program and a brilliant marketing campaign that targeted women as much as men. When perfected, the basic design was so successful that, with a few makeovers, it has lasted for over 70 years.

INNOCENTI ENTERS THE FRAY

Ferdinando Innocenti started his company in the 1920s to manufacture seamless steel tubing. Steady growth resulted in use of his product for aircraft and armament production. When Italy surrendered during the Second World War, he found himself in the same position as Enrico Piaggio, his factories in ruins behind enemy lines. Just like Piaggio, his ideas crystallised around providing the cheap transport that his shattered country so desperately needed. He commissioned Corradino D'Ascanio to design a prototype but the two men had disagreements about it: Innocenti wished to get his machinery humming quickly by using tubing for the chassis instead of D'Ascanio's spar frame. The designer was welcomed by Piaggio and the rest is Vespa history.

Innocenti then turned to Pier Luigi Torre, who also had experience in the aircraft industry. Torre's ideas were influenced by the Cushman 32 scooters he had seen and he approached the problem from a practical point of view without departing too far from the Cushman norm. After two prototypes, the design came together soon after the war ended. In theory the machine could be manufactured using existing processes but now Innocenti faced another problem. Not only was his factory reduced to rubble but it had been requisitioned and occupied by the Allied forces and he was denied access. Undaunted, he instigated a successful legal battle to regain possession and

begin the formidable task of building a new, if rudimentary, production line.

The many setbacks left Innocenti a year behind the Vespa, which was unveiled to great acclaim in 1946. The first of Innocenti's machines went on sale on 23 December 1947 to a mixed reception. It was called the Lambretta, which derived from the word Lambrate, a suburb of Milan.

The compact two-wheeler, known as the Model A, offered 4.1hp from a 125cc engine and was capable of 45mph with fuel economy of 110mpg. Unlike the avant-garde Vespa, the Lambretta's engine, fuel tank and glove box were visible and its overall appearance was relatively orthodox by comparison. To compensate, Innocenti offered the Model A in six colours — green, grey, blue, beige, red and maroon — to give his customers some individuality. What was not visible was the beautiful shaft drive contained within an oil-filled casing and representing new thinking. The downside was the virtual absence of suspension, with the sprung seat serving to smooth out the bumps.

In the first 12 months, 9,669 Lambrettas were produced and 9,000 were sold, leaving hundreds in the warehouse. Although this slower burn in sales, compared with the Vespa, was disappointing, Innocenti did not blink. Instead of reducing the price to shift the stock, he made the inspired decision to export the surplus to Argentina, the destination of many Italian expats. The Lambretta quickly won the hearts of new owners who were only too glad to own and drive this product from their homeland.

Meanwhile Innocenti's engineers started work on a new model. Improvements were made by moving the foot-operated gear shift to the handlebars, adding rear suspension, switching to larger-diameter eight-inch wheels, making provision for a passenger seat and offering a choice of four metallic colours. Designated Model B, the first example rolled off the line in November 1948. Backed up with an impressive advertising campaign and a newsletter entitled *Notiziario Lambretta*, production rolled on relentlessly. By January 1950 a total of 35,014 had been made. Innocenti had matched Piaggio for confidence and the following year granted the German company NSU a licence to produce Lambrettas. The motor scooters were beginning their global reach.

1947 LAMBRETTA MODEL A

SCOOTER WARS

By 1949 Piaggio and Innocenti had become serious rivals. At first they competed against each other with advertising campaigns that were successful in attracting women who had found new assertiveness since the war. With public demand expanding, the rivalry intensified as they strived for market share. Both were offering 125cc models with good fuel consumption and modest speeds of around 45mph. Piaggio and Innocenti then decided to change the perception of their products to impress the male population. They did this by successfully competing with motorcycles at circuits like Ospedoletti and entering into a duel for speed endurance records.

The objective of the endurance records was to achieve sustained speeds over set periods from one hour

1950 MONTLHERY VESPA

to 48 hours and set distances from one kilometre to 5,000 miles. The existing 125cc record was set in 1933 with an Aubier Dunne engine. At 49.7mph it was a soft enough target for an attempt to be made to claim a world record and create the kind of attention the two manufacturers were looking for.

Innocenti got off the mark first with a Lambretta Model A modified with fairings and the engine enclosed in an air scoop. In 1949 a 20-kilometre stretch of the Roma-Ostia motorway was chosen for the exercise, which involved slowing down and turning at each end together with stopping for fuel. The Model A triumphed with 13 records at speeds of up to 59mph. Innocenti went

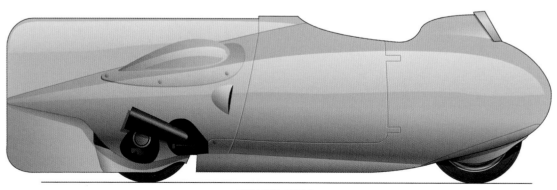

1951 VESPA SILURO

1951 INNOCENTI STREAMLINER

on to set more records at the Montlhéry speed bowl and relentlessly pushed average speeds to 78mph. They were certainly generating huge publicity.

Piaggio responded on 6 April 1950 with the streamlined Vespa Montlhéry and set 17 new world records in 10 hours, pushing speeds to 85mph. An irate Innocenti fought back to reclaim all the laurels with streamlining of his own and speeds up to 88mph. As a last throw of the dice, Piaggio fielded a fully enclosed streamliner shaped like a torpedo to attempt the outright speed record for the kilometre. On 9 February 1951 the Vespa Siluro hurtled down the Rome-Ostia Autostrada to record an average of 103mph and break the magic 'ton'.

The motor scooter had exceeded all

1949 LAMBRETTA ENDURANCE RACER

expectations but Innocenti wanted one more tilt. Needing more power, chief engineer Pier Luigi Torre fitted a small supercharger to improve the engine's volumetric efficiency at high rpm. This was installed in a streamlined body and developed over two months. On 8 August 1951, this ultimate scooter, piloted by Romolo Ferri, streaked down the Autobahn between Munich and Ingolstadt to record an average speed of 124mph. It was game, set and match to Innocenti — and the record remained unbroken for 16 years.

LA DOLCE VITA

The contest for records had reached its conclusion with both the Vespa and Lambretta punching above their weight in a domain normally reserved for motorcycles. The battle now intensified for sales both in Italy and abroad. Enrico Piaggio and Ferdinando Innocenti had arguably created a new form of transport that positioned their machines in a social/cultural context. Whether they had had the foresight to expect this is unknown. Probably they were pleasantly surprised at the effect on the public and decided to make the most of a new market that had suddenly evolved. To their credit they had the resolve to put profits back into the product and explore the numerous possibilities for the future.

The advertising campaigns were sophisticated for that time and focused on what are known as lifestyle or aspirational adverts today. The step-through design was user-friendly for young women wearing skirts and even young men could get on board without splitting fashionable tight trousers. Adverts and posters portrayed young Italian *fashionistas* who had more going for them than the Blackshirts — they

were more colourful for one thing. Often young couples were depicted engaged in a leisure-time activity and generally enjoying a better life. In Italy this particular experience became known as the '*La Dolce Vita*' — 'The Good Life'.

Of course '*La Dolce Vita*' was for the most part mythical even in Italy but then we do not always believe the advertising. Not everyone lived near the beach or the historic buildings in Rome. Looking at the vintage posters, any hardened scooter driver today

would wince at the lightweight shoes, flimsy hat and unprotected skin, wondering at the injuries that could be experienced by coming off the machine at even moderate speeds. This made no difference as the motor scooter filled the post-war vacuum to change the way people worked and lived. It also influenced style and fashion shoots to become a fashion icon itself.

Piaggio had come second in the racing contest but still gained valuable credibility. Now the company aimed to win the bigger battle and it had one advantage. Although the Vespa and Lambretta were similar in functional capability, the Vespa had more style. The production figures for Vespa showed a steep upward curve and within two years over 30,000 were sold. At this particular moment the United States began a financial aid programme, called the Marshall Plan, to help revitalise European economies, those of both friends and old foes. This gave an added boost to the scooter manufacturers and when Vespa production began at Hoffman-Werke of Lintorf in Germany under licence in 1950 figures topped 60,000. By 1951 the first imported Vespas in America were being sold by Sears under its 'Allstate' brand.

In 1953 Hollywood released a film called *Roman Holiday*, made on location in Italy. It starred Audrey Hepburn with

NSU Lambrettas were introduced to the American market.

Scooters preaching the gospel of Italian style were immediately embraced as a symbol of '*La Dolce Vita*'. They were soon crowned by the aftermarket

Gary Cooper, Anthony Perkins, and Jean-Paul Belmondo on their credits. Lambretta's hall of fame featured Jayne Mansfield, Debbie Reynolds, Laurel and Hardy, James Cagney, Rock Hudson, Bobby Darin and Gina Lollobrigida. A

GENE KELLY & BARBARA LAAGE   ROCK HUDSON & GINA LOLLOBRIGIDA   ELSA MARTINELLI   PAUL NEWMAN

Gregory Peck and featured a Vespa 125. The scooter became an American sensation and it is claimed that this Oscar-winning film helped generate 100,000 worldwide sales.

Lambretta, meanwhile, had not been idle. Its production figures were catching up fast with sales for the 12 months to November 1951 exceeding 100,000. That same year German-made

dentures of movie stars like Gene Kelly and enhanced by the graceful forms of silver-screen goddesses. The Hollywood *glitterati* were only too happy to take a photo opportunity with either of the machines. Vespa could boast Ursula Andress, Geraldine Chaplin, Joan Collins, Virna Lisi, Milla Jovovich, Marcello Mastroianni, Charlton Heston, John Wayne, Henry Fonda,

Lambretta was also presented to Prince Rainier and Princess Grace of Monaco.

As if this wasn't enough, the stylish Italian scooters featured in many more films that helped to establish their iconic status. It is hard to imagine a more effective marketing campaign. Enrico and Ferdinando must have rubbed their hands with glee at all this worldwide exposure.

A scene from the Hollywood film Roman Holiday

EVOLUTION

Piaggio and Innocenti had, in Italy at least, created a new species of two-wheeled transport. Now, to keep up the momentum, they had to adapt to the market. Piaggio had a head start with the 90cc Vespa. The benefit of the

Marshall Plan was that it also helped other industries to get back on their feet and so create new customers. Vespa was soon upgraded to a 125cc engine and by 1955 also offered a 150cc

option. That same year the Gran Sport or GS 150 was introduced and this was a different proposition entirely.

Ten years after the war ended the consumer was ready for more than the fairly utilitarian 40mph Vespas built

1955 VESPA 125 & 150cc

1955 VESPA GS 150cc

1962 VESPA GS 160cc

1964 VESPA SS 180cc

so far. The GS 150 refined the basic design with pleasing compound curves and hardly a straight line in sight. The enclosed handlebars were also a further step away from motorcycle convention. With a factory-tuned engine and a four-speed gearbox, it was capable of 60+mph and is regarded as the best-looking scooter Piaggio ever made. Even Lambretta owners grudgingly agree that aesthetically it has no peers.

There followed in 1962 and 1964 the GS 160 and the GS 180, capable of 62mph and 65mph respectively. Nice though they were, they did not quite equal the classic lines of the GS 150.

The Lambretta was mechanically

1950 TO 1958 LAMBRETTA LC & LD 125/150cc

1958 LAMBRETTA SERIES ONE Li 125/150cc

1959 LAMBRETTA SERIES TWO Li 125/150/175cc

1961 LAMBRETTA SERIES THREE (SLIMSTYLE) Li 125/150cc

sound but had a bit of catching up to do in the styling department. To this end the LC model was introduced in 1950. It was remodelled with full-size legshields and side panels covering the engine compartment, making it cleaner in appearance and operation. By this time both the Vespa and Lambretta had incorporated fan cooling of the engine — another departure from motorcycle practice. The three-speed LC was produced alongside the open-sided versions until the variant LD replaced all the previous models. The LC/LD models, in a choice of colours, were very successful with over half a million units sold but still looked lumpy alongside the gracious curves of the

Vespas, especially the GS 150.

The competition between Piaggio and Innocenti was as intense as ever so it was back to the drawing board to reinvent the Lambretta. Vespas were continuously reworked over the years but still retained the original visual concept. The Lambretta now underwent a fundamental change. The efficient shaft drive was replaced by an enclosed chain drive to reduce production costs and the cylinder barrel was repositioned horizontally. A new tube frame formed the basis and the side panels were a more pleasing curved shape. Enclosed handlebars were adopted but the headlight was still in a fixed position on the front

fairing. This new model was introduced in 1957 as the Lambretta Series One range and was available with a 125cc, 150cc or 175cc engine. It was soon replaced by the Series Two models with the headlight on the handlebars. This reworked engine/frame combination would see out the production run of all future models. Further bodywork restyling in 1961 resulted in the 'slimstyle' range which also offered a TV 200cc engine, capable of 70mph, for exports to the UK.

The slimstyle design was slightly restyled again and renamed the SX before the final model, the GP, was unveiled in 1969 and lost some of the earlier charisma.

1962 LAMBRETTA SERIES THREE (SLIMSTYLE) TV 175/200cc

1966 LAMBRETTA (SLIMSTYLE) SX 150/200cc

The Marshall Plan helped to revitalise Italian industry

NOW LET'S ACCESSORISE

Teenagers had not yet been invented during the early years of scooters and most people under the age of 20 had little disposable income, so early advertising in Italy was aimed at young adults in their 20s and early 30s. Single women were targeted as much as men and posters also often depicted young couples engaging in social activity. As the country recovered and there were a few more *Lire* to go round, the style-conscious Italians applied this ethos to their scooters. Following fashion is in itself a bit of an enigma. When it comes to the length of a hemline or the cut of a pair of trousers, most people prefer the latest fashion, even if it means they end up wearing much the same clothing but in different colours and patterns.

So it was with their scooters. They were not of a mind to deface their pride and joy with stripes or other graphics so turned to the accessory market. This offered a plethora of easy-to-apply aftermarket chrome extras — some functional and some purely decorative.

This became the means to personalise a scooter and give a sense of individuality. Front and rear racks had a practical use for carrying a spare

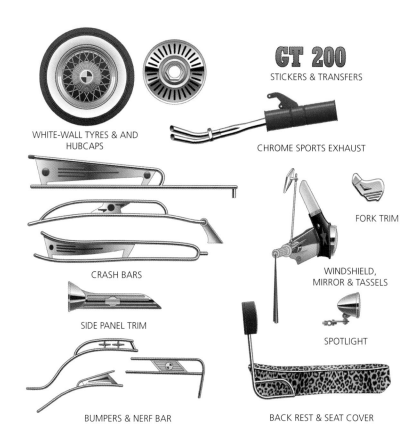

WHITE-WALL TYRES & AND HUBCAPS

GT 200
STICKERS & TRANSFERS

CHROME SPORTS EXHAUST

CRASH BARS

FORK TRIM

SIDE PANEL TRIM

WINDSHIELD, MIRROR & TASSELS

SPOTLIGHT

BUMPERS & NERF BAR

BACK REST & SEAT COVER

wheel or some light luggage. Attractive chrome crash bars also served a purpose by protecting the scooter in the event of an accident, helping to prevent panel-beating repairs and resprays. Mud flaps and windshields also gave practical service of sorts. Beyond the functional accessories came a multitude of purely decorative items like chrome hubcaps, whitewall tyres, chrome fork trims, handlebar tassels, decorative mudguard bumpers and pointless sport exhausts that just gave a more resonant sound. What all these accessories did was give the owners the chance to express themselves in different ways.

The Piaggio and Innocenti factories also produced accessories but on a larger and more practical scale. Pre-war Italian car output figures were a fraction of the numbers produced elsewhere in Europe and in the early post-war years the difference deepened. Ownership of private cars in Italy during the 1950s remained very limited, so Piaggio found many enthusiastic customers when it recognised a market need and produced a sidecar for the Vespa in 1948. The scooter had now become a family vehicle with room for three plus luggage. Innocenti soon followed suit and then produced a trailer. The

VESPA SIDECAR

extra carrying capacity allowed hotel or camping holidays for couples who wished to enjoy touring the country. The scooter's potential was opening up new markets and making possible a different way of thinking and living. With very low fuel consumption, scooters offered freedom and the simple joy of driving such a machine when the weather was pleasant.

LAMBRETTA TRAILER

PIAGGIO GOES APE

When scooter production was well underway, Enrico Piaggio turned his attention to the shortage of light transport vehicles and decided to fill the gap in the market. Corradino D'Ascanio came up with the solution in 1948 by creating the Piaggio Ape, a three-wheel utility vehicle based on the 125cc scooter. It is no surprise that it was named the Ape because this translates as 'bee' and it began to appear alongside its cousin the wasp. The Ape found immediate application as a delivery vehicle that helped to increase the sales of many retailers. Although

hailed as a brilliantly innovative idea, this was not the first such vehicle. In Japan the Mazda-Go, a three-wheel open truck based on a motorcycle, had been produced in 1931. This type of machine, known as an auto rickshaw, found a home all over south-east Asia.

Cushman also predated the Ape by producing the 1943 Model 53 three-wheel utility vehicle, adopted by the military in the Second World War, and no doubt noticed on air bases and army camps in Italy during the conflict. This was followed in 1947 by the Cushman Package Kar, for commercial use in

transporting and selling anything from Coca-Cola to engine oil.

However, there is no denying that the Ape came at the right time. Cheap to buy and economical to run, it was perfect for the economic climate in Italy at that time and the streets were soon full of busy bees going about their particular business. Having won a vote of confidence from the consumer, Piaggio began a never-ending quest for improvements to the concept. An enclosed cab was added and attention was paid to the driver's comfort by installing a heater and converting to a

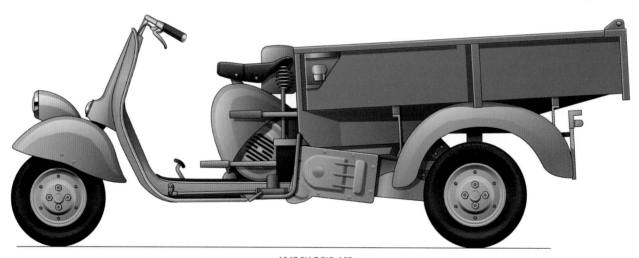

1947 PIAGGIO APE

steering wheel. From its original usage as a general delivery workhorse, the options became almost unlimited, such as specialised domestic delivery of paraffin or transport of farm produce. It was also adopted as a mobile shop selling products like bread, ice cream and coffee directly from the vehicle.

Improvements continued by moving the engine to the rear, offering petrol engine options of 50cc, 175cc and 200cc, plus a 422cc four-stroke diesel variant — together with updated styling over the years. Manufacture of the Ape also started in India in 2006 with an electric LV zero-emission model rolling off the lines in 2009. Production continues to this day with the diesel Ape Classic, a flat-bed pick-up truck with drop-down sides able to haul up to 805kg.

With a production run of 70 years and counting, Piaggio has proved with the Ape that the company got it right from the very start. It has contributed to the economic development of many countries around the world.

THE LAMBRO STRIKES BACK

Although the Lambro name was only introduced in 1963, it is generally used to refer to all Lambretta three-wheelers. Following Piaggio's lead with the Ape, Innocenti contested the market with a three-wheeler of their own.

The original prototype, the Lambretta FA, is lost in the River Lambro's mist and the first model available was the Lambretta FB. The 'F' refers to '*Furgone*' (van) and 'B' the series. There followed the FC and FD versions. In 1957 a cab or '*cabina*' was added and introduced as the FDC model with a 150cc engine. In 1959 the engine size was increased to 175cc and the new offering was presented as the Lambretta Li 175 Series 1. It featured four forward gears and one reverse but retained the handlebar steering. Next came the Lambretta Li 175 Series 2, which had a roomier cab and front and rear indicators.

At last, in 1963, the next new model was simply named the Lambro 175. It was sold alongside the Lambro 200, which had a larger engine and was capable of handling a 500kg load. At this point it made more sense to name the Lambros for their load-carrying ability so the Lambro 450 and 550 models came next.

The versatile Lambros found the same customers as the Piaggio Ape but Innocenti took things further by promoting 'Lambro Special Uses' and offering the Lambro as a chassis-only option to utility companies, government bodies and municipalities.

1949 LAMBRO FB

This opened the market for the manufacture of specialist bodies and the vehicle was adapted for use in refuse disposal, firefighting, street maintenance, postal services and port authorities. The Lambro also found practical application at hospitals and universities. One example above shows it in TWA livery for use by the airline.

Chassis-only exports led to further diverse use in other countries.

More variants followed through to the Lambro 600, which was the last model to come off the Innocenti production line. During the 1960s Innocenti had been producing the Mini under licence and by getting into bed with the 'sick man of Europe'

Innocenti sealed their fate. British Leyland bought the company in 1972 and sold the entire Lambretta manufacturing and trademark rights to Scooters India Ltd (SIL).

This was the end of the line for all Italian Lambrettas. Three years later British Leyland collapsed and the government stepped in to nationalise it.

THE BEAUTY WITH A DARK SECRET

The first practical two-stroke engine, as we know it, is credited to Dugald Clerk, *circa* 1880. The four-stroke engine, which fired the petrol/air mixture on every second upward stroke of the piston, had already been invented by Nicolaus Otto. Clerk's idea was to fire the mixture on every upward stroke and so develop twice the power. Clerk's long-stroke engine had the complication of an auxiliary piston and cylinder to provide the mixture at atmospheric pressure plus primitive poppet valves (See Fig.1).

Joseph Day took the concept forward in 1889 by using the crankcase to compress and transfer the mixture. To begin with he incorporated a flap valve on the piston crown and one in the inlet port. With a masterstroke by Frederick Cock, who worked for

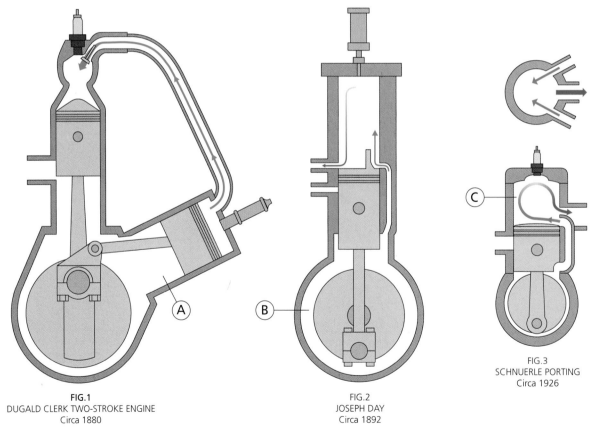

FIG.1
DUGALD CLERK TWO-STROKE ENGINE
Circa 1880

FIG.2
JOSEPH DAY
Circa 1892

FIG.3
SCHNUERLE PORTING
Circa 1926

Day, these valves were eliminated. By introducing a transfer port and moving the inlet port, the piston itself could control the passage of mixture — leaving only three moving parts. This required the use of a deflector piston to direct the fresh mixture towards the top of the cylinder (see Fig.2).

Next came Alfred Angas Scott, who started a motorcycle company in 1908 and adopted the Day two-stroke configuration. Scott took this further forward by altering the dimensions to make the bore and stroke of similar proportions to create a very compact short-stroke unit. His two-stroke motorcycles were very successful, achieving Isle of Man TT victories in 1912 and 1913. Further development saw the introduction of the Flying Squirrel in 1922. These machines were beautifully made but expensive, costing almost double the equivalent four-stroke price. The 600cc twin-cylinder layout with water cooling pumped out 24hp and was years ahead of its time.

While Scott was producing his high-quality motorcycles, Villiers was busy manufacturing more basic engines. In 1912 a single-cylinder 269cc two-stroke

1922 SCOTT FLYING SQUIRREL

engine was produced. By 1917 Villiers had invented the flywheel magneto, which eliminated the usual separate unit with its own drive. This made the engine self-contained and more compact. This engine was adopted by many long-forgotten motorcycle manufacturers of the day such as Sparkbrook, Wilkin and Hobart. The simplicity and low price of the unit made it an immediate success and led to three million Villiers two-stroke engines being sold in many different countries over the next half century.

The next big improvement came in 1926 when Adolf Schnürle improved cylinder filling by arranging the transfer ports either side of the exhaust port to direct the fresh mixture against the opposite side of the cylinder and up to the top (see Fig.3). This improved volumetric efficiency and made the heavy, heat-retaining deflector piston redundant, allowing a lighter flat top or slightly domed replacement. In turn this led to higher rpm and a more efficient engine.

The two-stroke engine had now reached a stage of development that was beautiful in its simplicity. With only three moving parts (crankshaft, connecting rod and piston), it had reached a stage of reasonable reliability and could hold its own against four-stroke engines of similar displacement.

During the Second World War, Villiers engines were used in the paratroopers' 98cc Welbike and the utility 122cc James ML (Military Lightweight) produced by The James Cycle Company Ltd. The ML was deployed in the D-Day operations of 6 June 1944. When a particular despatch rider who was used to bigger, four-stroke machines was asked what he thought of the little James, he replied that you wind it up and it goes — just like a 'Clockwork Mouse'. The name stuck. With fewer moving parts than a four-stroke, it was much easier to service and repair in combat conditions.

JAMES ML 'THE CLOCKWORK MOUSE' Circa 1944

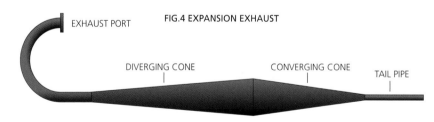

FIG.4 EXPANSION EXHAUST

EXHAUST PORT

DIVERGING CONE

CONVERGING CONE

TAIL PIPE

About 6,000 were supplied and gave stalwart service during the conflict.

The next two-stroke innovation was the expansion chamber exhaust, which became a quantum leap as far as power output was concerned. Early prototypes had first appeared on DKW racers in 1951. Walter Kaaden developed the idea to such an extent that his 125cc racing engine was eventually producing 25hp at 10,800rpm. The expansion chamber is both simple and complex.

At a glance it comprises just two cones and a couple of pipes welded together to form a hollow chamber — what could be simpler? The complexity lies in the relationship between all the dimensions. The exhaust pipe from the cylinder has to be a certain length and diameter. The first cone is divergent and helps extract the exhaust gases from the cylinder. The convergent cone creates a pressure wave to push any escaping fresh charge back into the cylinder and the tailpipe (stinger) vents the exhaust to the atmosphere. By altering the measurements, dramatic increases in power could be obtained but only within a certain rpm range.

Benefiting from Kaaden's work, Yamaha prepared a V4 125cc racer for the 1967 season. With ultra-high primary compression, pistons the size of cotton reels and radical cylinder porting, this machine won the 125cc world championship that year and the next. The engine produced over 42hp (more than many small cars of the period) at 17,000rpm but needed up to 12 gears to keep it in the high powerband — dropping to 12,000rpm would risk stalling.

The writing was on the wall for four-strokes. The 250cc and 500cc two-strokes were equally effective. The burst of power was so violent when they 'came on the pipe' that riders nicknamed them the 'Unrideables', but these heroes built up a love/hate relationship with the machines that dominated Grand Prix racing for nearly three decades. After their all-conquering dominance, the rule book was changed to place them at a disadvantage.

Back on normal roads, the two-stroke's ugly secret had been exposed. It was a dirty engine with unacceptably high emissions. The most common form of engine lubrication is to add oil to the petrol. Inevitably some of this oil is burned in the combustion

YAMAHA RA31A V4 125cc

process. Furthermore, the fact that the transfer ports and the exhaust port are open at the same time means that some fresh fuel is lost through the exhaust at periods in the rpm range. This made them worse offenders than some small

cars and so they have been gradually banned throughout most of the world.

Although poor emissions have painted the two-stroke into a corner, it

still refuses to go quietly. In 2008 the Buddfab Streamliner, created by John Buddenbaum and Eric Noyes, set a 50cc record of 144.891mph at the Bonneville Salt Flats. The following year they recorded 155.513mph in the

50cc BUDDFAB STREAMLINER

100cc class and 186.646mph with a 125cc engine. Only the very few will ever see these high numbers on any vehicle speedometer.

BACK TO THE FUTURE

When scooters are mentioned, the first names that usually spring to mind are the Italian Vespas and Lambrettas that became a global success from the 1950s onwards. Needless to say, they were not the first of the breed. For that we have to travel back in time to New York circa 1915 to find the Autoped. Reminiscent of a child's toy, it was as basic as it gets but everything has to start somewhere. An air-cooled 155cc engine was mounted over the front wheel with the clutch and brake operated by pushing the steering column backwards and forwards. The Empire Rubber & Tire Company supplied the distinctive red tyres and the claimed speed was 30mph. It was seemingly just a novelty for the well-off, with adverts depicting women bobbling over the cobblestones and presumably negotiating the horse droppings while keeping their long skirts off the ground, but it was also adopted by the US Post Office Service.

This novel mode of transport crossed the Atlantic to appear in Britain in 1917 for a photo opportunity with actress Shirley Kellogg in London's Hyde Park.

The idea caught on and it was not long before a dozen or so British companies that had been reliant on war work began to manufacture motor scooters. Most were poorly designed, unreliable and too expensive — so sales were low. One such company was Macklum, which introduced a 2hp model in 1920 complete with a sprung seat, but it only remained in production for two years. By 1924 all the other competitors had also disappeared.

While all these primitive concoctions were trying to make an impact, along

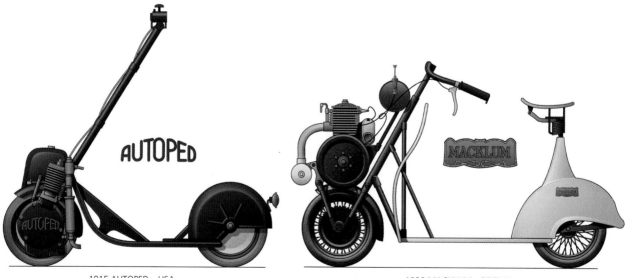

1915 AUTOPED – USA

1920 MACKLUM – BRITAIN

1920 UNIBUS – BRITAIN

came the Unibus conceived by Harold Boultbee and built by the Gloster Aircraft Company. This was a well-designed machine, decades ahead of its time, incorporating many of the features that would come to define the motor scooter in the 1950s. Built on a step-through frame with legshields and leaf-spring suspension for both 16-inch wheels, it featured alloy bodywork that concealed all the mechanical parts. Motive power was a single-cylinder 269cc two- stroke engine driving through a clutch and two-speed gearbox to a shaft drive.

1938 SALSBURY MOTOR GLIDE – USA

It even featured a starting handle on the dashboard. Although the Unibus was an advanced design and built to a high standard, it did not sell well because in was very expensive at 95 guineas, a year's wages for ordinary folk, and production ceased in 1922.

The early scooters did not quite get it right and disappeared from sight until, back across the Atlantic, American Foster Salsbury created the Salsbury Motor Glide in 1935. The first-generation version had no clutch, gearbox or suspension and was push-started, which meant that every time it stopped another push start was necessary. Fortunately it only weighed 65 pounds. Nevertheless many Hollywood celebrites wanted one, including movie stars like Judy Garland and Paulette Goddard. With a speed of 20mph, it was more of a fun item that was good for delivering newspapers or whizzing around film sets and it only sold in the hundreds. Improving the breed, Salsbury introduced an automatic clutch, a four-stroke engine and an automatic transmission for the 1938 Model 40 Motor Glide. This was something of a technological wonder at that time and is the configuration for most modern twist-and-go scooters today.

Soon after starting up, Salsbury faced stiff opposition from Cushman, which offered the Auto-Glide in 1936 to increase sales of its Husky engines. Three years later Hayward and Channing Powell launched the Powell Streamliner, which was favoured by American troops during the occupation of Japan at the close of the Second World War. These three offerings looked similar with provision for just one person.

Back in Britain again, during the war a small two-wheel vehicle was requested by Station IX (the 'Inter Services Research Bureau') for use by the Special Operations Executive (SOE). As a result the Welbike was born and was so secret that it was named after the town where it was built — Welwyn. As it turned out, the SOE did not have much use for the Welbike but the

1939 POWELL STREAMLINER – USA

Paratroops did and so it found its way into Italy. The Welbike does not exactly fit the definition of a scooter but its use of a 98cc two-stroke Villiers engine with integrated flywheel magneto was similar to the thinking of Piaggio and

Innocenti. The Welbike was also deployed in the airborne assault on Arnhem during Operation Market Garden but the idea fell on stony ground in starving Holland.

In the USA the Cushman company had more resources and financial muscle than its competitors. The Military Model 32 became the basis for the next generation of domestic scooters. The Model 50 was introduced in 1945 to predate the Vespa by one year. Production output steadily improved to a peak of 15,000 in the late 1950s but then increasing competiton arrived

1942 WELBIKE – BRITAIN

from imported scooters and Cushman got left behind. The company stopped building scooters in 1965.

The Powell Streamliner had already disappeared by 1950 but left a legacy on the other side of the world. In the aftermath of Japan's surrender, industrial giants were forbidden from producing armaments. The country faced a similar situation to that in Italy. The Nakajima Aircraft Company was dissolved and the Fuji Sangyo Company was created. Salvaging what they could from the debris of their factories, they decided to address the country's pressing need for cheap, economical transport. Many of the occupying American troops had brought Powell Streamliner scooters with them. This design was carefully studied and then copied to become the basis for Fuji's first scooter called the Rabbit (S1). The desperate need for improvisation was shown by using an aircraft tail wheel for the front wheel of the scooter. The Fuji Rabbit began rolling

1945 CUSHMAN MODEL 50 – USA

out of the factory six months before the first Vespa and became an instant success with the public.

Although the wartime damage to

1946 FUJI RABBIT S1 – JAPAN

Italy was severe, it was much worse in Japan. It is widely known that the cities of Hiroshima and Nagasaki were wiped out by atomic bombs. What is not so well known is that extensive destruction was inflicted on over 60 other cities by B-29 bombers that were largely unopposed in the later stages of the war.

Mitsubishi, which had produced the Zero fighter plane, also decided to produce scooters of its own by cloning the Salsbury Motor Glide. The result was the Silver Pigeon, which remained in production for 17 years, with over 450,000 examples made. Filling the roads with Rabbits and Pigeons was functional rather than cultural but is regarded as a significant factor in revitalising the post-war Japanese economy. As a postscript, these machines were exported to America some ten years later and contributed to the decline of scooter manufacturing there. Together with cars, cameras and other advanced high-tech products, the Japanese proved that economic success could be attained without military aggression.

In the meantime Cushman was still trucking on with production of its Package Kar, which predated both the Piaggio Ape and the Innocenti Lambro. It was based on the Model 39 military utility vehicle seen during the war and used for delivering light goods such as Coca-Cola and motor oil over short distances. Cushman was one of the few American companies allowed to continue production of vehicles for the domestic market during the Second World War. This was because both petrol and tyre rationing had been introduced, and scooters were more

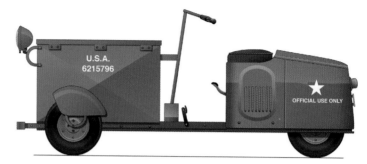

1943 CUSHMAN MODEL 39 – USA

1947 CUSHMAN PACKAGE KAR – USA

BAJAJ TUK TUK TAXI – INDIA

economical. The concept of affordable and cheap-to-run three-wheel vehicles has since found a ready market around the world.

Although Cushman finally ceased production of scooters in 1965, the company's influence on three-wheel versions has been far-reaching. Their descendants, the Lambro and the Ape, have found their way to many different countries, earning the nickname Tuk-Tuk from the sound of their small two-stroke engines, and they have spawned many imitators. The original auto rickshaws in the Far East became difficult to keep in service when Japanese manufacturers ceased production of spare parts in 1960. More modern variations appeared in places like Bangkok in Thailand, now the Tuk-Tuk capital of south-east Asia, where part of the attraction for tourists is to take a tour in a Tuk-Tuk blasting out their favourite rock music.

This genre is known by numerous names — Tuk-Tuk, Toktok, Tik-Tik, Bajaji, Moto Taxi, Cocotaxi, Beep-Beep and many more. Nowadays these vehicles are a common sight in Africa, the Middle East, most of Asia, Central America and South America — and even in parts of Europe. The endlessly useful Tuk-Tuk is more prevalent in countries with a tropical or sub-tropical climate because they are not usually fully enclosed. Along with all

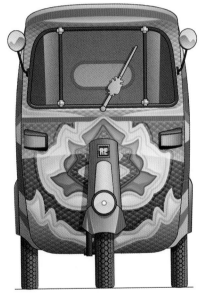

ALL-PURPOSE BAJAJ TUK TUK – INDIA

the normal duties, Tuk-Tuks are also very popular as short-distance taxis or tourist mini buses. Piaggio continues to produce the Ape and opened a factory in India in 2006. That country is also home to Bajaj of Pune, which produces around 750,000 Tuk-Tuks per year.

It is impossible to guess how much influence the Tuk-Tuk has had on the countries where tourism is a major part of their economies.

As is to be expected, pressure has been brought to bear on cleaning up Tuk-Tuk emissions in recent years, with legislation introduced for LPG-fuelled options and electric versions that do not pollute city streets. As of 2018, India has about 1.5 million battery-powered Tuk-Tuks on its roads with 11,000 new ones every month. The days of petrol, diesel and even LPG are numbered.

In the western hemisphere Portugal has also made great strides and is now regarded as the European e-Tuk centre with electric versions used for tourism.

It would seem logical that this type of electric vehicle will gradually become more prevalent in the western world. After all, that was how milk was delivered for decades, and the British company Morrison-Electricar even produced electric trucks capable of carrying 1.5 tons for short-haul delivery way back in the 1930s.

It has all been done before but with modern technology maybe we can go back to the future — only better.

GETTING IN ON THE ACTION

The post-war scooter boom saw many competitors enter the expanding market. While the Unibus, Vespa and Lambretta were created by designers with aeronautical experience, who were conscious of efficient construction and power-to-weight ratios, most of the rest were not. This section is a selective gallery of the good, the bad and the ugly — with a special category for the faintly ridiculous.

Seven months after the first Vespa came off the line in Italy, the Swallow Gadabout appeared in Britain in 1946. Most two wheelers were exported at that time to help Britain's foreign exchange deficit but the Gadabout

1946 SWALLOW GADABOUT – BRITAIN

was available in the home market for essential services. It entered service with the Staffordshire, Warwickshire, Leicester and Walsall police and provided transport for District Nurses.

Fitted with a 125cc Villiers engine, it was underpowered and overweight, only managing about 30mph. It went out of production in 1951.

In America the streamlined Salsbury Model 85 appeared. It was big and heavy but represented an advanced design equipped with an adequate 320cc four-stroke engine and continuously variable transmission (CVT) that predated every twist-and-go scooter available today. This 50mph Cadillac of scooters missed a social function as it had only one seat but its ample storage space found favour with companies such

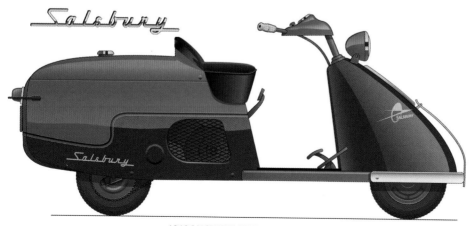

1946 SALSBURY MODEL 85 – USA

CORGI

1948 BROCKHOUSE CORGI – BRITAIN

like a scooter but was really a heavily disguised motorbike and failed in both categories. Weighing more than twice as much as an Italian scooter, it featured plenty of weather protection but this also created more wind resistance. The original 150cc engine was not up to the task and was upgraded to 175cc and then 200cc. The forward-placed engine did not allow a step-through but made room for ample storage space under the rear seat. Nicknamed the 'Dustbin', it did not sell well and by 1958 was

as Western Union as a delivery vehicle. The innovative Salsbury Motors proved that timing is everything by going out of business in 1947 just as the scooter boom got underway.

Britain's Corgi Motorcycle Company was formed in 1946 to produce a civilian version of the Paratroops Welbike. A similar 98cc two-stroke engine was used with a petrol tank placed between the handlebars and seat. Many examples were exported to America before the model became available on the home market in 1948. It was not particularly suited to everyday use yet 27,000 were sold before it faded away like an old soldier in 1954.

German company Maico's approach to the challenge was quite different.

The Maico Mobil, marketed as a car on two wheels, may have looked vaguely

1950 MAICO MOBIL – GERMANY

consigned to — guess where?

The Bastert-Werkes in Germany followed the same train of thought as Maico to produce the Einspurauto, which meant 'Single-track car'. It also missed the point but in a more elegant way. Construction involved alloy bodywork over a steel frame and solid aluminium wheels. Beautifully made, the Einspurauto, at 2.25 metres long, was oversized, overweight, underpowered and overpriced. It was beyond the reach of much of the population and only 1,200 units were sold during its four-year production run. This failure in the

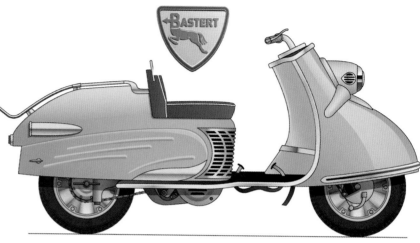

1951 BASTERT EINSPURAUTO – GERMANY

market has made it a rare and sought-after machine today.

Inspired by the Vespa, German

1951 GOGGO – GERMANY

Andreas Glas decided to produce a scooter of his own. This time most of the essential scooter parameters were met. Initially the 125cc engine was inadequate and this was upgraded to 150cc and then 200cc (with 10hp). The combination of weight, power, speed and fuel consumption was a workable solution and the price was within reach of prospective buyers. The Goggo was a success and 46,000 were built before production was switched to cars. This scooter did look as if it was modelled on some sort of armoured vehicle but with a name like Goggo all is forgiven.

The next German contender, manufactured by Zündapp, gets a wooden spoon in the beauty contest.

1953 ZUNDAPP BELLA – GERMANY

Naming it the Bella (for 'beautiful') hardly made up for its clumsy lines and large front mudguard. Beauty, however, is in the eye of the beholder and this design has many admirers. Zündapp's experience in making motorcycles is evident in the Bella's configuration. It has large wheels, an external chain drive and an air tunnel for engine cooling that prevents a step-through facility. A 146cc two-stroke engine was upgraded to 198cc to eventually push this reliable heavyweight to 60mph. It was good enough to reach sales of 130,000 over a ten-year period.

Heinkel stepped up the competition in 1953, setting out its stall by naming its scooter the Tourist. As with all the previous hopefuls, it was aimed at the younger adult market. Looking suitably Teutonic, it was built for comfort and reliability. With a few extras as standard and an electric starter, it weighed in at 330lb and, unusually for a scooter, it was equipped with a four-stroke engine, upgraded from 149cc to 174cc. Although it was more expensive than the Vespa and Lambretta, it gained a reputation as the ideal touring machine. When imported by Britain and America it was described as the 'Rolls-Royce' and 'Cadillac' of scooters respectively. Approximately 163,000 units were produced in a decade.

The 1954 Moto Rumi Formichino was a work of art from the very beginning.

1953 HEINKEL TOURIST – GERMANY

1954 MOTO RUMI LITTLE ANT – ITALY

Company boss Donnino Rumi was an accomplished sculptor who fashioned the bodywork sections in clay to create moulds from which aluminium panels were cast and bolted together to form a lightweight monocoque shell with the engine as an integral part. A precision-made 125cc twin-cylinder two-stroke engine was designed by Pietro Vassena. Moto Rumi's creation was a winning combination on and off the road. With a little development, it was capable of over 85mph and won the famous Bol d'Or 24-hour race at Montlhéry in France in 1957, 1958 and 1960 against motorcycle opposition. Yet even this little beauty did not last the distance as Moto Rumi ceased production in 1960.

The year of 1954 also saw the introduction of the Piatti scooter, which made a transition from the sublime to the ridiculous. Designed by Vincent Piatti, it was first made in Belgium by D'Ieteren. Featuring a short wheelbase, an inefficient 124cc two-stroke engine, a three-speed gearbox and a single-support dual seat, it has been described as the worst scooter ever designed with comments ranging from 'amusing' to 'hideous'. Looking more like a pet robot from a sci-fi TV series and boasting a top speed of eventually 38mph, it was safer staying indoors than taking its chances on busy roads. Cyclemaster in the Britain took up production in 1956. Finding few customers, the less than epic Piatti story ended the following year.

1954 PIATTI – BELGIUM

Noting the success of the Fuji Rabbit and Mitsubishi Silver Pigeon, Honda set its sights on a piece of the action and cut its teeth on a first scooter — the Honda Juno. It featured an electric starter and introduced glass-fibre bodywork and indicator lights, but the end result was too heavy for its four-stroke engine, making it slow off the mark and limiting top speed to only 43mph. It was also too complicated: even the full-screen windshield, complete with sunshield, was over-engineered. Last but not least, the Juno was too expensive, so production reached only 6,000 examples and

1954 HONDA JUNO – JAPAN

ceased after 18 months. Yet this was a classic case of 'if at first you don't

succeed, try, try again', for Honda is now one of the world's largest scooter producers and its market share in India alone exceeds 50%.

In 1955 the Dayton Cycle Company entered the scooter market and introduced the oddly named Albatross. This British-made ugly duckling was similar to the Bella which, along with the Heinkel, was an obvious competitor. The Albatross featured an air tunnel for cooling its 225cc Villiers engine, which was soon upgraded to 250cc to give an optimistic claimed top speed of 70mph. Regardless of Dayton's boasts, this scooter did not

1956 DAYTON ALBATROSS – BRITAIN

1957 CEZETA – CZECHOSLOVAK SOCIALIST REPUBLIC

hot exhaust in the event of hitting a vehicle in front. Some 4,000 were also assembled in New Zealand. CZ must have got most of it right because with little more than a minor makeover the Cezeta returned in 2017 as a modern electric scooter.

The British company DKR was founded in 1957. Its first scooter, the Dove, was powered by a 147cc Villiers engine. Next came the Pegasus and then the Defiant with a larger 197cc Villiers engine. They all had the same styling but the Defiant featured a four-speed gearbox and electric start with a top speed of 60mph. This body style

have much style and was outsold by the Italian machines. By 1960 the Albatross had become extinct.

The Cezeta was manufactured from 1957 to 1964 in the Czechoslovak Socialist Republic by CZ. Designed by motorcycle racer Jaroslav František Koch, it was powered by a 175cc two-stroke engine giving a top speed of 55mph. Although described by observers as either a torpedo or a pig, it did have a certain pizzazz considering that it was built behind the Iron Curtain. It had a large tunnel in the footwell area, storage space under the seat and a fuel tank integrated into the

front mudguard, which seems a quick way for petrol to make contact with a

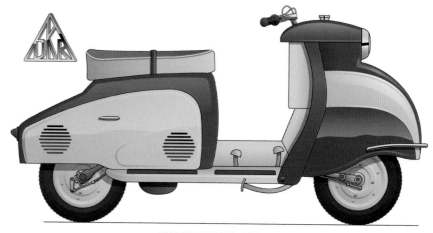

1957 DKR DEFIANT – BRITAIN

1958 CAPRI – ITALY

a motorcycle-style external chain and weighed about 200lb. The range was expanded to include other engine sizes of 50cc, 80cc, 125cc and 150cc, but even the largest engine was never going to make this the intrepid adventurer's choice. Like many small scooters, this one was aimed at women, but Agrati's competitors had such a strong grip on the Italian market that most sales had to come from elsewhere.

In Britain the Sun Cycle & Fittings Company Limited had marketed its first motorcycle in 1911. The decision to produce a motor scooter in 1959 resulted in a strange case of mistaken

was hardly a class act: who were they trying to impress with that bulbous front end? Sales were initially good enough to keep the company afloat even though these scooters, with their external chain drive, were already yesterday's models. Seeing the light in 1960, DKR introduced a new scooter called the Capella, which looked more like the Lambretta configuration, but it arrived too late and the company folded in 1966.

Back in Italy, Agrati tried to get in on the action with the Capri. Faced with intense competition from the Vespa and Lambretta in its homeland, Agrati had to do something different. Its first attempt was a neat and tidy three-speed

with a 70cc engine (even smaller than the first Vespa's engine) producing a mere 3.8hp, so the model was really only suitable as a 'runaround'. It retained

1959 SUN WASP – BRITAIN

1959 TRIUMPH TIGRESS – BRITAIN

1963 FUJI RABBIT 150 – JAPAN

identity. Styling the rear end vaguely like a Lambretta with a front end borrowed from the Albatross, Sun chose the name Wasp — after the Vespa. Yet again Villiers Engineering was kept busy providing the 174cc motive power. To accomodate the female driver, the Wasp had a low saddle height, narrowed footboards and an easy-to-operate foot pedal gear change. Sun's effort did not make much impression on the market and few examples were sold. By 1961 this Wasp was gone for good, making it another sought-after rarity today.

The BSA-owned Triumph Company unveiled its first scooter in 1959. This was a nice machine with fluid lines and a tail section that looked even more like a wasp than the Vespa. As Triumph already produced a motorcycle called the Tiger, it opted to name its new scooter the Tigress, which probably alienated a few prospective male buyers; the model was also sold as the BSA Sunbeam. Fundamentally a good design, it was produced when Britain was entering a period of industrial strife with outdated manufacturing practices. Delivery difficulties and a reputation for unreliability contributed to unimpressive sales. Two engine sizes were offered: the 175cc two-stroke produced less power than equivalent Vespas and Lambrettas, while the 250cc four-stroke twin eliminated enthusiastic 16-year-olds because it could not be driven on a provisional licence. Having missed the marketing bullseye, production of the Tigress ceased in 1965.

After the enormous success of Japan's first scooter, the Rabbit S1, Fuji developed a new generation of Rabbits. Incorporating electric starters, automatic transmissions and pneumatic suspension systems, they were the first Japanese scooters capable of 60mph. These were very sophisticated scooters for their time and a wide range of over 25 different models was offered for the Rabbit 150 and the Rabbit 125. Production ran for 20 years until Japan's industrial expertise proved to be its nemesis. The economy had expanded and saw the arrival of the 'Kei', a breed of affordable small-displacement mini cars. Scooter

demand decreased and Fuji switched to production of the 350cc Subaru Kei car. The last Rabbit scooter was made on 29 June 1968.

Scooter sales in the western world also declined as post-war economies recovered. Small cars were appearing

at more affordable prices within the reach of young adults taking on hire-purchase agreements. The era of touring scooters like the Heinkel, pictured on the poster shown on this page, was coming to a close.

The Italian paradigm had proved to be the best combination of overall

performance and style, taking the lion's share of the market. Now-defunct companies manufactured numerous other forgotten scooters and all experienced widely varied levels of failure. In Britain, Royal Enfield's Villiers-powered contender was modestly named the Fantabulous but it proved to be anything but, and left little trace. The Velocette Viceroy of 1960, an over-complicated design with an opposed twin-cylinder engine, managed to find only 682 buyers during a period that saw sales of Lambretta's Series 2 range exceed 250,000. Other scooters from the past include the Achilles, Bernadet, Diana, Hercules, Iso, Jawa, Lohner, Monark, Tempo and Walba — to name just a few.

It is hard to imagine how so many could have got it so wrong! And yet there have been avid fans to keep examples of most of these machines in roadworthy condition even while a new scooter dawn was rising in the East.

CHEAP AND CHEERFUL

Britain in the 1950s was enduring what were called the Years of Austerity. Food rationing lingered until 1954 and National Service continued until 1960. At the beginning of that decade there were only four million vehicles of all kinds on the road — a number that has since increased nine-fold. Few people owned a car or even aspired to do so. Apart from the well off upper middle classes, private motor vehicles were the domain of doctors, estate agents and sales representatives lucky enough to have a company car. There was little of what is now described as disposable income. Even professional footballers travelled to matches on public transport along with their fans.

The idea of *La Dolce Vita* was a mythical lifestyle only experienced by cinemagoers watching Italian or Hollywood films. The reality in rainy Britain was quite different. Even so the need for affordable transport was just as strong as in the rest of Europe. This was the perfect time for the motor scooter. A few homegrown products began to make an appearance but a big impact was made by imported Italian Vespas and Lambrettas.

MIDWIVES AND SCHOOL TEACHERS ADOPTED THE ECONOMICAL SCOOTER

THE REALITY IN BRITAIN WHEN GOING ABROAD FOR A HOLIDAY WAS A FANTASY

Far away from the glitter of Hollywood, the British public were treated to advertisements featuring the emerging rock 'n' roller Cliff Richard or Miss World plus the *Take Your Pick* game show offering a scooter as the star prize. As the pictures on this page show, the riders were a world away from the bikini-clad girls that so often featured on sun-drenched Italian posters. This was no deterrent and a good market developed. Scooters found many appreciative customers from midwives and district nurses to schoolteachers and country dwellers, all of whom found that they offered big advantages over a bicycle. As well as older owners the perennial young couples were attracted and the scooter also served in fleets to deliver newspapers and various other goods.

After a slow start, sales grew to the point where, in 1953, the new Lambretta LD 150 became so popular that the initial quota imported from Italy quickly sold out and French-built versions were needed to meet demand. The secondhand market that duly developed would attract a very different kind of customer in the next decade.

RALLY TO THE PENNANT

Aside from the grind of commuting to work in traffic and poor weather, scooter owners found that driving their machines in clement conditions could be a great pleasure. The scooter boom resulted in the formation of the participants having a common interest in scooters, the open air and social interaction. Those taking part were young adults up to the age of about 35 with a high proportion of female drivers. These owners were covers, the idea of defacing them with stripes or other graphics did not enter their minds. This was soon to change in the next decade.

Seaside resorts were often the chosen venue. As many as 3,000 would gather

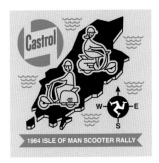

1964 ISLE OF MAN SCOOTER RALLY

the Lambretta Club of Great Britain in 1953. This was so successful that Lambretta Concessionaires created its own club called the British Lambretta Owners Association. The UK-based Douglas Company, which had contracted to both import and build Vespas, also encouraged Vespa clubs. The different clubs were supported with the newsletters *Vespa News* and *Lambretta Leader*. A multitude of clubs began to appear with names like the Bromley Innocents and the Vagabonds, with their own badges and pennants.

Various rallies were organised with proud of their scooters and although they embellished them with a few chrome accessories and tartan seat

A WOMAN RALLY ENTHUSIAST STANDING NEXT TO HER 1959 LAMBRETTA SERIES ONE Li

at Brighton or Southend to take part in fun events such as treasure hunts and social evenings with a soundtrack of 1950s rock 'n' rollers Tommy Steele and Marty Wilde. Destinations varied from places like St Albans and Hunstanton to the Isle of Man. The Camberley Lucky Seven Club even organised a display team that toured the country and other events included obstacle courses and a fancy-dress ball for 700 enthusiasts. Popular rallies to Whitby, Tenby, Kelso, Weymouth, Woolacombe and Southport continue today, with the biggest one, on the Isle of Wight, attracting up to 5,000 historic machines.

LAMBRETTA CONQUERS THE UK

Enrico Piaggio had a firm grip on the scooter market, not just in Italy but across Europe and eventually throughout the world, so the Vespa consistently outsold the Lambretta — except in Britain. Why was this?

Douglas, a Bristol-based motorcycle company dating back to 1907, made a contractual agreement with Piaggio to manufacture Vespas in Britain, starting in 1951. Part of the deal gave

Douglas the exclusive franchise to sell Vespas not only in Britain but also in Commonwealth countries, thereby saving Piaggio the work involved in exporting and marketing Italian-made machines to these parts of the world. On the surface this seemed a reasonable idea but closer scrutiny would have revealed that Douglas was in a perilous financial state. Slow to get off the mark, Douglas's output was always lower than Piaggio expected. The quality of the product was also questionable. This made Britain the only country in the world where Lambretta gained the upper hand. Enrico was disappointed by this state of affairs but resigned himself to this unwanted outcome.

Meanwhile, an opportunity was spotted by father and son James and Peter Agg of south London. In 1951, the year the first Vespa rolled off the lines at Douglas and the Swallow Gadabout ceased production, the Aggs set up Lambretta Concessionaires and began to import Lambrettas directly from Innocenti, starting with 500 C and LC models. In the beginning it was difficult to make any real impact especially as the scooter was a relatively

new idea and met with a fair amount of dealer resistance.

In Britain it was generally accepted that all motorised two-wheel vehicles were motorcycles and all cars had rear-wheel drive. One can almost hear the unspoken words, 'It has always been that way and will always be that way.' Many were soon to be evicted from the comfort zone of these fixed notions.

James Agg was near retirement age when he took up the challenge so son Peter became the driving force. In contrast to the dire efforts at Douglas, the younger Agg displayed at least two qualities that the rival company lacked — faith and enthusiasm. James began the job of convincing established dealers that it was in their interests to stock his scooters and Lambrettas soon began to appear on British roads. Taking leaf after leaf from Enrico Piaggio's book, Peter pressed home the advantage. The British Lambretta Owners Association was inaugurated, supported by the *Lambretta Leader* newsletter. A network of 1,000 service stations was set up nationwide, each with a full inventory of Lambretta parts. Workshops were equipped with

used to doing their own maintenance.

The indefatigable Peter Agg supplied dealer signs, point-of-sale material and servicing price posters. The arrival of a new model was preceded by trips to the Milan factory for dealers to view it in advance. The public then got their first sight at the Lambretta stand at Earls Court, suitably impressed by giant hoarding advertisements on their way in.

Peter Agg's boundless energy paid dividends as his booming business repeatedly beat off numerous rivals that never got it quite right. By the end of

the decade he had made the Lambretta the strongest-selling two-wheeled vehicle Britain had ever seen — and established the country as Innocenti's biggest foreign market.

One of Agg's many marketing ideas was to customise models that were soon to be superseded. This resulted in the Rallymaster, a Series 2 Li 150 treated to black stripes on the side panels and a turning front mudguard as on Spanish models. Uprated cylinder porting, a large-bore carburettor and a performance exhaust were augmented with a rev counter to complete the job.

the necessary special tools and the mechanics went through Lambretta training programmes. Dealers quickly realised the increased revenue of servicing and repair work especially as there was now a high proportion of women customers, whereas before motorcyclists were usually male and

1961 LAMBRETTA CONCESSIONAIRE SERIES TWO Li 150cc RALLYMASTER

RACING LAMBRETTAS

Piaggio may have achieved the highest global production figures but Lambretta took ownership of a different set of numerals — the ones with mph after them. After Innocenti came out on top in the head-to-head speed battles of 1951, this particular race continued with private owners.

The Italian Ancillotti brothers, Alberto and Piero, prepared a stripped-down 202cc Lambretta for speed trials at Monza in 1965 and set a standing-start quarter-mile time of 14.8 seconds, a performance that would have given many a 500cc motorcycle a run for its money. The following year the brothers squeezed into a Fiat 600 with the scooter strapped to the roof and headed to Elvington airfield in the north of England. With their projectile's engine now enlarged to 228cc, they set more records for both the standing-start quarter-mile and kilometre, completing the latter at a terminal speed of 106mph. Using only modified factory parts and running on petrol, it was a stunning performance.

There was also a British contender at Monza in 1965 by the name of Marlene Parker with a Lambretta prepared by

ANCILLOTTI STRIPPED-DOWN LAMBRETTA SPRINTER – Circa 1965

Filtrate and Lambretta Concessionaires. This scooter, named the Atlanta V, was even more radical than the Ancillotti machine. Cut down to the minimum height and with clip-on handlebars attached to the front forks, it was a

FIG.1 GENERIC LAMBRETTA KNEELER CONFIGURATION – Circa 1965

1972 FRED WILLINGHAM LAMBRETTA SPRINTER

configuration described as a 'kneeler' (see Fig.1). The Atlanta V story is dogged by false claims but Parker failed to break any records due to various technical problems. However, for a young woman to even attempt to drive such a formidable machine at high speed was enough to make Parker's name legendary.

Fred Willingham, a teenager from Bradford, was inspired by watching visiting American drag racers and decided to get involved himself. Choosing a cheap Lambretta as a starting point, he opted for the 'kneeler' layout with a 175cc engine and named his creation 'Trip Trap'. Its début in 1965 surprised many

regulars and eventually 'Trip Trap' set a standing-start quarter mile time of 16.5 seconds to beat all the competition. When engine displacement was increased to 225cc, handling problems arose and led Willingham to switch in 1968 to a stretched Lambretta Series 2 frame that was named 'UPU2' and continued his steep learning curve.

MARLENE PARKER ON ATLANTA V REPLETE WITH A FULL FRONT FAIRING

With little access to sources of information and using only hand tools, he began to modify everything on the scooter and left no stone unturned for the next four years. Clutch, barrel, piston, cylinder head and carburation all came under close scrutiny. The only thing lacking was a high-performance expansion exhaust but this technology was still in its development stage.

Willingham then teamed up with Peter Ham, an RAF engineer, and the pair gained access to enough equipment to take their ideas even further. Soon seven-plate clutches appeared, followed by the installation of a Japanese piston. The frame on Fred's machine was changed again to a Series 3 Lambretta, cleverly modified to allow a down-draught Wal Phillips fuel injector to be fitted together with a custom-made cylinder barrel that increased capacity to 250cc. By this time Fred had also traded added weight for a full front fairing. The sum total of all this dedicated effort put Willingham in a class of his own.

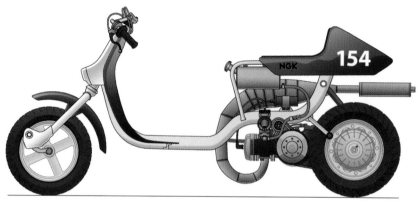

FIG.2 GENERIC LAMBRETTA SPRINTER – Circa 2000

At a sprint meeting at Fulbeck in 1972, Willingham set a new record for the standing-start quarter mile at 13.95 seconds, an unbelievable achievement that few supercars of the day could match. Not content with this, he achieved a top speed of 112mph over the flying mile. These records became the benchmark for Lambretta sprinters and stood for over ten years. The quarter-mile time was finally beaten in the mid-1980s by John Scrutton and Richard Baker. Fred Willingham's unwanted machine ended its days in a scrapyard in 1990. One of the most historic Lambrettas ever built was gone forever — but the Willingham legend lives on.

Scrutton and Baker had helped to create the now accepted form of Lambretta sprinters (see Fig.2). Stuart Owen took note and by 1998 had joined the National Sprint Association (NSA) and began to make an impact. In the new millennium Ray Saxilby took on the engine-tuning duties and standing-start quarter-mile times dipped into the 12-second bracket with a terminal speed of 102mph. By 2002 Owen had collected five consecutive NSA championships, set a best quarter-mile time of 12.71 seconds and a speed of 117.3mph over the flying mile.

The ante was upped in 2009 when Keith Terry, who had previously recorded a 12.7 second quarter-mile on his highly modified Kursaal Flyer Lambretta sprinter, set another record

ERIC COPE'S 127MPH LAMBRETTA GP

SPRINTING ACTION AT ELVINGTON

BSSO CIRCUIT RACING ACTION

at Elvington airfield with a speed of 132mph over the flying mile. This was achieved without any streamlining. The powers of comprehension were further stretched to the limit on 5 July 2020 when Eric Cope managed to power a full-bodied, street-legal Lambretta GP

to a speed of 127.591mph at Elvington.

Sprinting and speed trials are not the only scooter sport activity. There is also an active programme of serious circuit racing across the country. This evolved from the reliability trials in the sixties that were organised by scooter clubs.

The desire for out-and-out racing grew to the point where this wish was granted in the early 1970s under the direction of the Federation of British Scooter Clubs. The NSSA (National Scooter Sport Association) evolved to take the sport further and the two organisations merged to become the BSSO (British Scooter Sport Organisation).

The racing takes place at various circuits around Britain and is organised by the BSSO into different classes. The Group 4 Lambrettas are based on stock model machines with restrictions on engine modifications but they can nevertheless achieve up to 98mph. Group 6 allows more extensive modifications and engines up to 260cc. This group regularly reaches speeds of up to 110mph on the straight at Snetterton circuit in Norfolk.

These Lambrettas are anything up to 57 years old, making them some of the very few historic machines, of any kind, that race head-to-head at nearly double their designed speed with three times their original horsepower.

There is no sign as yet that these high-performance scooters are going to go quietly into retirement.

GENERIC BSSO GROUP 4 LAMBRETTA CIRCUIT RACER

THE MOD PHENOMENON

The emergence of Mods was set against the background of post-war Britain. The cities were blackened by a century of coal smoke and the last of the national servicemen were only discharged in 1963.

The failure of many British manufacturing companies to reinvest saw them gradually left behind by resurgent industries in West Germany and Japan. Most men wore dark-coloured suits with a white shirt and a tie — even at Cup Final matches. Parents dressed their older children as a mirror image of themselves.

Amid this bleak environment various minority groups existed. The Teddy Boys liked rock 'n' roll and effected an Edwardian style of dress with drape jackets and thick crepe-sole shoes. Beatniks favoured a casual style with sloppy jumpers and beards while listening to Dizzy Gillespie. Modernists wore 'bum-freezer' suits and also liked modern jazz. Rockers rode motorcycles, wore black leather and drainpipe jeans. Like the Teds they favoured rock 'n' roll.

When Britain limped into the 1960s, the music fare consisted of pseudo-British rock 'n' roll clones and older-generation favourites like Perry Como. Originally rock 'n' rollers themselves, The Beatles hit the headlines in 1962 and put the lid on all previous styles

AMERICAN ARMY KOREAN ISSUE M-51 PARKA

by writing their own material. With unprecedented success, they quickly became the housewives' favourites, leaving the way open for other new music influences.

Although Britain is at least five hours ahead of America, it always seemed five years behind. America was seemingly the land of plenty where everyone had a fridge and a TV. They had invented the word 'teenager' and this had entered the British lexicon. In the early 1960s the phrase 'mod cons' appeared, meaning modern conveniences. The Beatles were soon wearing 'mod' collarless suits. This use of the word 'mod' is as an adjective and of course the Beatles were not Mods. It is accepted that the culture started in London not Merseyside.

This background created a situation in which a new sub-group of teenagers rejected all that had gone before. They wanted their own identity in clothes, music, dancing and transport. The result was the spontaneous appearance of Mods. Some time in 1963 the word 'mod' changed from an adjective to a noun. Their sudden appearance was described by Irish Jack, who frequented the Goldhawk Club in Shepherds Bush where he used to watch a group called The Detours. He said that one minute they were ordinary blokes and the next thing they were all Mods. It happened overnight like an electric current being switched on. The following year The Detours providentially decided to changed their name to The Who.

Back then there were no mobile phones, text messages, emails or social

media. Fewer than half of households had a telephone with many relying on the phone box at the end of the street. The Mod idea spread rapidly by word of mouth to become an underground movement that soon numbered many thousands of adherents. For transport the stylish Italian Vespas and Lambrettas were the only choice. The scooter boom of the 1950s had put many of these machines on the secondhand market when their original owners moved on to cheap cars. With a good work ethic, money could be saved for an older model. Alternatively advantage was taken of the newly introduced hire purchase system to buy a new one, providing an adult could be found to sign as guarantor.

For clothes, Mods turned away from the existing staid conformity and wished to differentiate themselves from other sub-groups. To this end department stores and high-street fashions were ignored. American Army M-51 fishtail parkas, first used in the Korean war, were discovered in army surplus stores. These were found to be ideal for protecting clothes while driving a scooter. Heavy-duty Levi jeans were found in Millets, a camping shop. They were as stiff as a board and were bought one size up to allow for shrinking. After being washed many times, the dark blue dye slowly lightened to a more acceptable colour. The Ben Sherman Company opened its doors in 1963. Its American-style, button-down, soft-collar shirts, which were offered in Madras cotton, were sought out in small independent shops. Fred Perry tennis shirts found a new life with these teenagers. The high-street tailor Burton provided mohair suits made from stock patterns in any chosen colour. Details like the lapels, vents, pocket flaps and number of buttons could be altered at customer request, at an affordable price or 'on tick' (payment by instalments).

LAMBRETTA SERIES TWO 150 – Circa 1965

1957 LAMBRETTA LD MK3 125

1959 LAMBRETTA SERIES ONE 150

Early choices for shoes were desert boots, brogues or leather Italian loafers.

Music was also sought elsewhere. The bland fare in the hit parade was rejected in favour of harder-edged black American rhythm and blues. This category was originally a catch-all term for all black music in segregated America, where R&B was relegated to black radio stations and charts. The music ranged from the blues to Motown and the gospel soul of Otis Redding. A love of dancing took a new turn by eliminating the necessity for a partner: boys and girls dancing on their own or in groups was normal.

The average age of the original genesis quickly gravitated downwards to 15-year-olds who adopted Mod style and aspired to owning a scooter on their 16th birthdays because it could be driven with a provisional licence. This differentiated them from all other social groups. No two Mods looked quite alike and it was the same with their scooters. The result was a kaleidoscope of visually different Vespas and Lambrettas.

No one knows who was the first to paint stripes on a scooter, but dislike

of the bland original factory colours led Mods to personalise their rides. This could vary from backyard brush-painted colours and stripes to the use of aerosol spray cans or professional paint jobs. Seat covers and chrome accessories completed the basic transformation. Accident damage simply created a new style. Mangled mudguards were replaced with alloy versions and side panels were simply removed. The addition of some decals might complete the look.

Scooters gave these baby-faced teenagers a new-found freedom that sidestepped public transport, freed them from the tyranny of the last bus or train, and spread the word even faster as they went where they pleased.

Much has been written about Mods over the years and certain myths are now seen as fact. In fact few scooters of the day were festooned with clusters of lights and mirrors. Not many Mods took pills and danced all night at the Scene Club in London and few could afford to buy new tailored clothes and the latest imported R&B record every week. At 16, many were still in education, had low-paid jobs or served

DOUGLAS VESPA 150 – Circa 1964

LAMBRETTA SERIES ONE Li 150 – Circa 1965

LAMBRETTA SERIES TWO Li 150 – Circa 1966

in this section are actual scooters remembered from the 1960s.

If someone in the family worked in the paint shop at London Airport, they might end up with a very nice Lambretta Series 2 Li 150 (top left) with an enamelled maroon respray complete with stripes. With a great deal of patience, a few rolls of masking tape and some aerosol spray cans, an old Lambretta LD (top right) could sport some chequered side panels like no other.

Dealers would often make an older Lambretta Series 1 TV 175 more visually appealing by chroming the front mudguard and side panels to contrast with a dark blue paint job, adding whitewall tyres for good measure (bottom right).

The idea of customising took flight and before long there were hundreds of personalised scooters parked outside big dance halls and Palais on a Saturday night sporting graphic stripes, glittering chrome and the RAF roundels. Copper-plated panels might also appear together with highly polished alloy parts. Dealers played their part by adding flashes even on new scooters

apprenticeships and could not afford the now stereotyped legend, although they certainly aspired to it.

Priorities were simple. The idea of driving a Bella or even the Italian Capri was laughable. It had to be a Vespa or Lambretta. After that a ticket to see a live band on a Saturday night and at least the minimum wardrobe was only

just within reach. Clothes, scooters and music were not the sole ownership of any part of society but the way the Mods put the combination together created a unique lifestyle that was instantly recognisable.

Personalising their scooters required some creativity, ingenuity and improvisation. All of the examples

LAMBRETTA LD 150 – Circa 1964

LAMBRETTA SERIES ONE TV 175 – Circa 1965

to make them more saleable. This kind of customising had no precedent in Britain with few cars displaying even the simple stripes that might be seen on racing cars of the period.

As a cultural group the Rockers, known to the Mods as 'Greasers', revelled in their reputation as ton-up boys although only larger motorcycles were capable of that speed. A fair amount of banter passed between the two groups. Typically the Rockers, who were generally older, would regard the Mods as long-haired and effeminate, ridiculing their scooters as hair dryers. Paradoxically the Rockers with their swept-back pompadour hair styles sometimes had even longer hair than the Mods and their BSA Bantams and Triumph Tiger Cubs were hardly a match for some of the faster scooters. The two groups usually went to different places socially but in 1964 the newspapers sensationalised scuffles at seaside resorts when they came into close conflict. The country was gripped by moral panic and the Mods were dubbed aggressive. Subsequently these clashes were few and less press-worthy than many other young groups judging

FINDING RADIO LUXEMBOURG ON THE MEDIUM WAVE FREQUENCY

by football crowds and student riots.

The movement had a profound effect on British culture that has lasted to the present day. At the time the BBC had a monopoly on radio broadcasting with the Light, Home and Third programmes, all aimed at adults. The only way to listen to teenage music was to tune in to Radio Luxembourg, broadcast from a country where there was little interest in it. When daytime radio had finished, the station was given over to the early disc jockeys who played popular records after 6.30pm. Teenagers in general demanded more and some entrepreneurs came up with the notion of using old ships to broadcast outside the three-mile limit, and so Radio Caroline and Radio London pirate stations were born. These initiatives brought American R&B to the youngsters in general and the Mods in particular.

Initially the means to listen to this music was the old valve radio found in every home, but the advent of the transistor radio meant pirate stations could be heard anywhere. Records were played at home on mono record players or even a radiogram.

Back in Shepherds Bush The Detours were heavily influenced. Now known as The Who, they adopted the Mod style. In East London The Small Faces were already Mods before they became famous. Three of them later joined Rod 'The Mod' Stewart to form The Faces. Favoured bands included The Rolling Stones and The Yardbirds, and other groups that cut their teeth on hard-edged R&B included The Pretty Things. Georgie Fame and The Blue Flames were another favourite that introduced crowds at the Flamingo and the Marquee to up-tempo R&B and Jamaican Ska music, known as Blue Beat after the British record label that released it. Berry Gordy's Motown output was released in Britain by the Tamla-Motown label, featuring The Four Tops, The Temptations, Marvin Gaye, Smokey Robinson, Martha and the Vandellas and The Supremes among others. All of these were in great demand. Other black American

artists on record labels like Stax, Chess and Atlantic found themselves brought into the fold.

The Mod influence extended to TV when *Ready Steady Go* first appeared on British screens. This ground-breaking show featured an audience of Mods dancing between heavy cameras. Groups featured were not restricted to the top 20 in the charts. Notably, The Who appeared on the programme more often than any other band.

Another Mod favourite, blue-eyed soul singer Dusty Springfield, created and introduced the *Ready Steady Go* 'Motown Special' in 1965 on which The Supremes, Stevie Wonder, The Miracles and Martha and the Vandellas experienced the kind of rapturous reception that they never received in America. In 1967

Stax records ran a tour of Britain with Otis Redding, Sam & Dave and the MGs, Arthur Conley, Eddie Floyd, The Mar Keys and Carla Thomas, who all received a fanatical welcome and stayed in hotels that they could enter through the front entrance. There were

some Mods who parked their scooters outside the Hammersmith Odeon to watch Otis and company and would claim it was the greatest moment of their teenage life. American Geno

Washington was based in Britain with his Ram Jam Band as was Jamaican Jimmy James and the Vagabonds. Both these performers earned a reputation as the hardest-working and most popular bands in the country.

To embrace black culture in this way put the Mods a long way ahead of the rest of the country when it came to racial equality. As champions of artists like Aretha Franklin, James Brown and Otis Redding, Mods recognised the excellence of these stars long before they were accepted by mainstream audiences.

Tastes in clothes and music could vary, beyond the common denominators, in London and later in the rest of the country. There was no Mod regulation handbook but the total effect became more than the sum

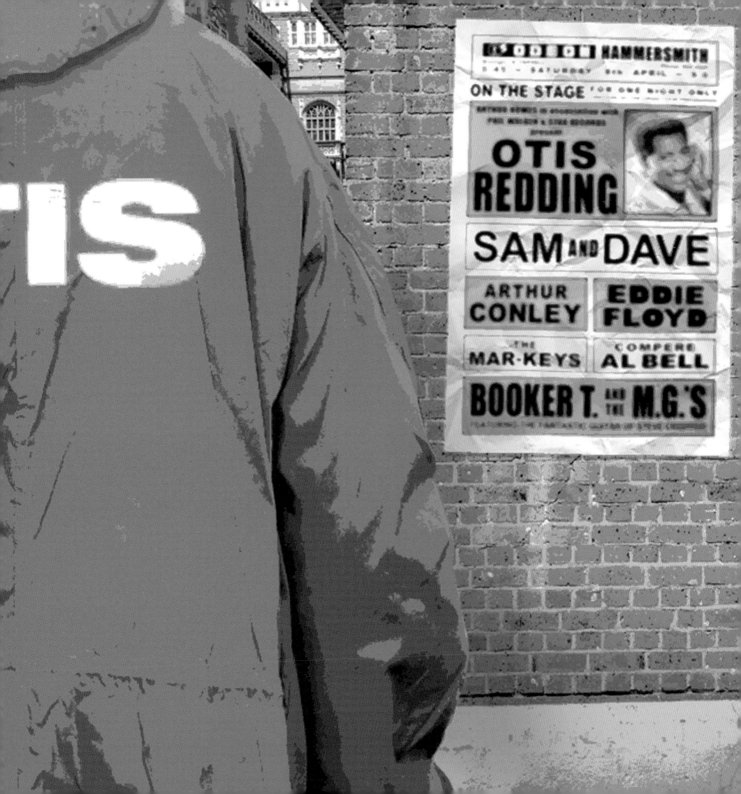

LAMBRETTA SERIES THREE TV 220 – Circa 1968

LAMBRETTA SERIES THREE TV 200 (EARLY VERSION) – Circa 1964

of the parts. The influence extends to today nearly 60 years later. The iconic status of the Vespa and Lambretta was assured. Black American R&B music became the foundation for much that followed. The clean-cut Mod style has been adopted by actor Martin Freeman and multiple Olympic medallist Bradley Wiggins, both of whom are a long way past their teenage years. Even Mod revivalists in Tokyo have captured the original and unmistakable look.

The tastes in customised scooters also varied. Some Mods were more interested in speed. The Lambretta TV 200 shown on this page (top left) was bored out to 220cc, received a fuel injector and dispensed with an air filter. An Ancillotti performance exhaust and some tuning of the cylinder barrel together with a slightly larger rear tyre added to the significant increase in its performance capability.

In another example, the stock Mark 1 TV 200 (bottom left) with its Li panels,was a resale. The original white colour was treated to some tangerine flashes that accentuated its classic lines, creating something that was beautiful in its simplicity and yet still capable of

LAMBRETTA SERIES ONE Li 164 – Circa 1967

VESPA GS 160 (DAMAGED FRONT MUDGUARD AND SPARE WHEEL BLISTER) – Circa 1966

reaching a top speed of 70mph.

If funds were tight, measures could be taken to try to keep up with the latest top-of-the-range machines. The 1959 Lambretta Series One 150cc shown here (top left) was stripped of all but the essentials to reduce weight. The engine was tuned and bored out to 164cc. A Wal Phillips fuel injector was installed together with an expansion exhaust. Startling acceleration was the result even if it could not quite match the top speed of the TV 200.

Accident damage gave a particular Vespa GS 160cc (bottom left) a unique style of its own. Removing the crumpled mudguard made a feature of the Vespa aircraft-style front forks. Scraped and dented side blisters were discarded to display the engine on one side and reveal the spare wheel on the other. A cheap imitation seat cover and crash bars completed the effect. Like Mod attire, it was the same but different.

All these machines and thousands more were in daily use for going to work or college. In the evenings the freedom of travel allowed friendships to develop and endure beyond a few streets away. Friday and Saturday saw

LAMBRETTA SERIES THREE TV 200 – Circa 1967

VESPA GS 160 – Circa 1968

them parked in colourful rows outside dance halls and small music venues. Sunday afternoons were often the time for gatherings at a friend's house to listen to records by artists like The Spencer Davis Group, Fontella Bass and Wilson Pickett.

Innocenti itself was even influenced by Mod culture to the extent that the Series Three TV 200 (tagged as the GT 200) was produced specifically for the British market and sported a colourful custom flash. Few of these machines were sold in Italy.

The Series Three TV 200 shown here (top left) is an example of the small number that were overdressed at the time. Only a few owners thought that the expense of the extra clutter was worthwhile but they contributed to the myth because the press preferred to have them at the front for photographs. Authentic photographs, easily identified by the lack of crash helmets, will show that most scooters were not overly adorned.

The Vespa GS 160 was introduced in 1962. This one (bottom left) features a later resale paint job in yellow and green and was paid for by hire purchase. Its proud owner used it to cruise to the Ilford Palais on a Saturday night.

The GS 160 was replaced in 1964 by the SS 180. The one on this page (top right) was originally white but was treated to a professional respray four years later to make it easier to sell.

The SS 180 was rated at 65mph and never matched the TV 200 Lambrettas, which were then replaced by the Lambretta SX 200 in 1966.

Stylish though the SX 200 was (the standard version is shown bottom right), it did not quite capture the charisma of earlier models and was rarely treated to the same level of customising.

Within a few years Mod culture and the scooter boom passed its peak and so did the halcyon days of American and British R&B when there seemed to be something new every week.

In the years since those exciting days there has been much discussion about the pros and cons of Mod culture, much of it by people who were not there at the time. But what is certain is that in the 1960s they made their own unique contribution to the scooter community that has since embraced the globe.

VESPA SS 180 – Circa 1968

LAMBRETTA SX 200 – Circa 1969

SIZE ISN'T EVERYTHING

Piaggio's first Vespa had a small 90cc engine that was upgraded in stages to 125cc, 150cc and on to the 160cc first introduced in 1962 and then updated to the SS 180's 180cc in 1964. Lambretta followed a similar pattern, starting with a 125cc that grew to 150cc, 175cc and then, in 1963, 200cc to meet demand from Britain although this model was not sold in any numbers in Italy. Both companies were doing very well but Piaggio was ahead of the game. With constant reinvestment and excellent advertising and marketing campaigns, Piaggio had established a firm grip on its home market.

Enrico Piaggio then spotted an opportunity that would help to consolidate his company's position. As young couples began turning to small affordable cars like the Fiat 500 or bubble cars, he decided to exploit legislation that allowed anyone from the age of 14 to drive a 50cc vehicle without a licence. The result was the Vespa 50, the last Vespa to be designed by Corradino D'Ascanio. Launched in 1963, it provided a new, small, easy-to-handle frame design with just one seat to comply with regulations that prohibited

taking a passenger. Promoted with the slogan 'Young, Modern and — without documents', it introduced the joys of scootering to a new, untapped strata of teenagers. It became a landmark in the history of the Vespa and three million

have since been manufactured.

Slow off the mark, Lambretta produced the J-Range. The first of the series was the 100cc Cento, which discarded the tube chassis of previous models and used the pressed-steel frame concept that Piaggio had adopted from the start. However, the 100cc engine ruled out the younger end of the teenage market. Being lighter, lower and narrower, with shorter handlebar levers than the earlier models, it was proportioned specifically for the average-sized woman. In 1965 it was replaced by a 50cc single-seat version

1963 VESPA 50

76

1964 LAMBRETTA J-RANGE CENTO

frame style of the very first models, it looked very space age for its time. The Bertone-designed machines were available as the Vega or Cometa 75cc versions in Britain. With good timing the Luna was launched in 1968, the year before Neil Armstrong took his giant leap for mankind. Considering it still looks modern today, the range was not a huge success with only 37,000 examples produced.

In these rapidly changing times, Lambretta itself soon faced the unforeseen fate of extinction.

but it was underpowered, offering only 1.5hp. Further improvements were tried but the J-Range did not do well with only 110,000 produced before it went the way of all Italian Lambrettas.

When the first Italian scooters appeared, liquid-fuel rockets were in an early stage of development in Germany. At the end of the war the German scientists were spirited away to America and by 1968 had helped to create the means to land a man on the moon. With this monumental feat imminent, Lambretta launched the Luna range.

Although reverting to the open-

1968 LAMBRETTA 75 VEGA

THE TIMES WERE CHANGING

Life inexorably moved on and with it came change, for better or worse — as the fashion industry was to show. By 1968 the Mod era was coming to a close and many of the reasons for its existence were fading away. It was essentially a teenage culture and those who had been involved at the outset were entering adult life with the responsibilities of marriage, children and mortgages. Understandably, later 16-year-olds wanted their own identities in terms of fashion and music.

The chemistry that was part of the Mod ethos was changing. The Mod-influenced *Ready Steady Go* was aired for the last time on 23 December 1966. Pirate radio stations were outlawed in 1967. Otis Redding died on 10 December 1967. The London-based British R&B bands had run their course: The Yardbirds disbanded in

1968, followed by The Small Faces in 1969, and then The Rolling Stones temporarily lost their way. Even The Who were beginning to distance themselves from the original fans who had made their name. British R&B was slowly being replaced by Psychedelic, Glam and Progressive Rock.

Over in America, as the Civil Rights Movement gained momentum, the Motown performers wished to sing more politically aware lyrics instead of the boy/girl dance music that had made them famous, and so another era

LAMBRETTA GP 125/150 & 200 – introduced in 1969

78

came to a close. Their girl singers from Baptist backgrounds either faded away or pursued stardom on a bigger stage.

Money also ruled back in Britain as small venues closed and promoters put bands into big halls and eventually stadiums. As Britain became a little more affluent, long-playing (LP) records began to sell in bigger quantities than singles — and small cars became more affordable on hire purchase.

At this time the last of the classic Lambretta Slimstyle TV/SX range rolled off the production lines in 1969, to be replaced by the Lambretta GP designed by Nuccio Bertone. Although improvements were made to the engine and ignition, the new model was just a makeover visually. Offered in the single colours of turquoise, white, orange, red and yellow ochre, it had factory-applied 'sporty' stripes on its side panels. Bertone also introduced matt-black plastic fittings that influenced future car designers and he used a trendy ink-splat graphic on the front fairing. The end result was a machine with modern styling but no charisma.

New youth cultures had appeared, including Hippies and Flower Children.

Dancing in small smoky clubs was replaced by head-banging at open-air concerts. Horsepower was exchanged for flower power. For the most part these new youth cultures were peace-loving. They found their fashions in flea markets with no restrictions on colour or style and enjoyed their time while it lasted. For many it was just a passing fashion. Others attempted to

make a genuine difference by seeking to change social values.

The Mods had outlived their time and began to fade away. The scooters went with them, consigned to rust quietly in back gardens, garages and sheds. What teenagers thought of as a way of life could only survive in their formative years. But, as it turned out, affection for scooters was to live on for much longer than anyone could ever have imagined.

RETURN OF THE ROUNDEL

By the mid-1970s demand for scooters had dwindled to the extent that ten-year-old models changed hands for as little as £10. These same machines, even in poor condition, are worth thousands today. Uninterested in other youth

movements at that time, many young lads took advantage of the market and a resurgence of scooter Mods began to occur. Like the original movement, it was inescapably entwined with clothes and music. Some of the original Mod style was adopted, including the parka.

Music was a different proposition. The emergence of British R&B along with Motown, Stax and Atlantic performers in the 1960s could not be repeated — you had to have been there. One solution was to look past mainstream Motown hits and go for the lesser-known recordings of that period. This provided a new portfolio of songs that had not been widely

heard and became known as Northern Soul. The British music contribution came predominantly from The Jam. As with The Who, founder member Paul Weller adopted a Mod appearance and went so far as to buy a Lambretta. This gave him the platform, again like The Who, to write lyrics that allowed him to talk to his audience rather than just sing at them. This reawakening was given a further boost by the release of the film *Quadrophenia*, which gave an accurate

depiction — albeit in 'condensed-milk' form — of what some of the original Mod teenagers, yet to reach maturity, had been doing in the previous decade. Taken together, all of this was enough to consolidate a new Mod renaissance.

As a result the roundel graphic returned. Originally devised as a recognition symbol for RAF aircraft, it became synonymous with Mod culture. The early 1960s saw the advent of Pop art and more focus on graphic

JIMMY – LAMBRETTA SERIES THREE Li 150

images. Many large companies had spent heavily on simplifying their logos to make them instantly recognisable in the interest of what is now known as 'brand awareness'.

No one knows who was first but, without any committee meetings, the roundel began to appear. Fabric was stitched onto T-shirts or even ties and it was hand-painted onto scooter side panels and the back of parkas. The roundel became one of the simplest

and most effective cultural graphics of its day and will forever be associated with Mod culture. It reappeared on posters for *Quadrophenia*, on promotional material for The Jam and on 'mod-revival badges'. Since then it has been extensively used by clothing

companies and to advertise scooter aftermarket products — a particular kind of brand awareness that has proved most effective.

This time around, Mods and scooters, having attained iconic status, were to last a lot longer than expected. This happened not only in Britain but spread in various forms far around the globe. As a result, a great many of the favoured Italian Vespas and Lambrettas have been saved from extinction and show no sign of going the same way as the kaftan, beads and afro hairdos. Over half a century later they have, in fact, inspired love and affection in yet more people of all ages.

THE FACE – VESPA GS 160

THE RISE OF TWIST-AND-GO

When Salsbury introduced automatic transmission on the Model 40 Auto Glide back in 1938, it was such a good idea that only 24 years passed before any other scooter manufacturer caught on. An automatic system eventually reappeared in Britain in 1962 when Triumph introduced the Tina, which had continuously variable transmission (CVT) and a centrifugal clutch.

Designed as an easy-to-ride shopping vehicle, the Tina was aimed specifically at women. However, it was plagued with technical problems from the outset and in particular the drive had a tendency to jam and immobilise the machine. As a British product, it was technically inept and became a laughing stock. An improved version was offered in 1965 but sales were poor and it was discontinued in 1970. So Triumph missed its golden opportunity to conquer the global scooter market.

The CVT transmission replaced manual gear-changing and gave a smoother ride. It worked by means of a belt drive between two pulleys that could automatically adjust their diameters to give variable drive ratios (see diagram). In the right hands it was

TRIUMPH TINA 100 – From 1962

CONTINUOUSLY VARIABLE TRANSMISSION

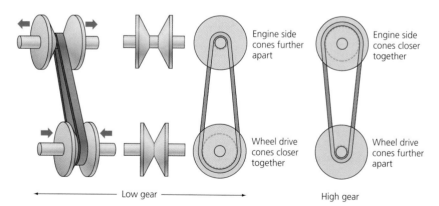

Engine side cones further apart

Wheel drive cones closer together

Engine side cones closer together

Wheel drive cones further apart

Low gear

High gear

The transmission uses two pulleys. Each pulley consists of two cones. When the cones are moved closer together they increase the effetive diameter of the pulley. When they are moved further apart they decrease the effective diameter of the pulley. In this way the gearing is made continuously variable.

to have a huge impact.

Honda had suffered disappointment with the Juno back in 1954 but introduced its own two-stroke CVT scooter in 1983, 45 years after the Salsbury Model 40. Named the Honda Lead, it met with great success in different engine sizes. Honda then invested heavily in Peugeot and the Kinetic Motor Company in India, both manufacturing Honda's scooters. In 1999 Honda launched the four-stroke CVT Activa in India and never looked back. Honda can now claim to have manufactured every second scooter in

HONDA LEAD 125 – From 1983

KYMCO SUPER 8 50 FOUR-STROKE – Circa 2018

India and the total exceeds 20 million.

Both the Honda Lead and Activa followed the accepted Italian-inspired look of a scooter. However, as a consequence of the relentless demand for something different in today's world, a new configuration appeared. The Kymco CVT 50cc four-stroke is typical of this new breed, complete with factory-applied graphics. Still a scooter, it shows motorcycle influence with its angular looks and kicked-up tail. Kymco has become the largest scooter manufacturer in Taiwan and the fifth largest worldwide.

THE UK PRESERVATION SOCIETY

After the scooter resurgence in the late 1970s, the future of the classic Italian machines was assured. Different factions have since developed enough affection to keep them alive in roadworthy condition. These vary from senior citizens who have sought to buy what was once the object of their teenage desire to Mod revivalists and the culture of Scooterboys.

These groups do not necessarily follow the same music or clothing styles but they all have two-stroke Italian

EXAMPLE OF A MODERATE CUTDOWN

scooters in their blood. Scooterboys have no great affinity with the first generation of Mods and favour their own style. There are no rules but the MA-1 bomber jacket is a favourite, often covered in event patches, but the main focus is the scooter — which they have taken to a different level.

The average age for these groups is much higher than the teenagers in the 1960s and they have more disposable income to lavish on treasured Lambrettas and Vespas. Time-honoured customising with stripes, chrome and accessories has since been enhanced with complex and

ARTIST'S IMPRESSION OF A SCOOTER MURAL

expensive murals covering any subject from Motown idols to Japanese Koi carp or Pharaohs. Even chaincases and alloy parts on the handlebars have been treated to intricate engravings. With aftermarket performance engine parts such as barrels, pistons, carburettors and exhausts, some machines are capable of an easy 80mph in street-legal form. The earlier stripped-down versions have been taken further by 'cutdowns', which can feature extended chopper-style forks and bobbed tails as seen on the previous page.

Since the first scooter revival, enthusiasts have kept the passion going for over 50 years. The preferred models are pre-1972 Italian Vespas and Lambrettas, and other types continue to be regarded with the disdain that has always prevailed. The Lambretta Club

of Great Britain boasts 5,000 members and over 100 other clubs exist. Together with owners not affiliated to clubs, the total number of classic scooters in Britain is estimated at nearly 40,000.

Anything built before 1980 is now described as an 'historic' machine. In this context these scooters enjoy special status. Because scooters are so much cheaper to buy and renovate than cars, there are large numbers of them in excellent and roadworthy condition. Another unusual factor is that customising and tuning does not necessarily make much difference to values compared with standard versions. The scooter scene is alive and well with regular rallies that attract thousands of owners each year. From teenagers to pensioners, the common bond is strong enough to keep these marques alive for some time to come — and for some devotees it provides a valid excuse to wear the iconic parka.

RUST RESURRECTION

The affection for old scooters in Britain means that more and more historic examples are appearing on the road. Many are still being discovered rusting in sheds, garages, barns and back gardens. Some come onto the market when a long-time small museum calls it a day or a compulsive hoarder finally decides to cash in his chips for retirement. It is also possible to find a specimen loitering in a scrapyard waiting for someone to pay the over-the-top asking price.

There are scooters imported from various parts of the world. Lambretta GPs were manufactured in India until 1998 and many worn-out, battered examples have been brought back for renovation, with demand high enough to lead to waiting lists. There have also been scooters imported from Italy, Spain and elsewhere.

This constant demand is replicated throughout the world. There are barn finds in America and Australia and many derelict scooters in scrapyards in Indonesia. Lambrettas are like hens' teeth in the United States so anything uncovered there is likely to find a good

home. Other machines are turning up across Europe.

The Vespa is the most dominant brand across the globe but in Britain the Lambretta rules the popularity stakes. Such is the devotion to these scooters that a great many aftermarket

suppliers have sprung up to meet every demand. It is now possible to bring many a forlorn hope back to life. If an abandoned and cannibalised frame is found, it can be returned to its former glory as long as it is not terminally afflicted with rust and the frame number is intact. Even bent frames can be straightened. Bodywork

items like the fairing and side panels are available as new steel pressings or glass-fibre substitutes. From replacement handlebars to the engine and rear hub, everything is catered for by specialist suppliers. If a 'find' is accompanied by some period documentation, then an original or age-related number plate can be registered.

Although the Vespa is not quite as well served, there is still a vast catalogue of available parts and it remains possible to bring one in reclaimable condition back to its former glory.

For the immediate future all seems well for these icons of the breed — but times do change. Compared with the era in which these scooters were made, we are now much more concerned about the environment. Many countries have brought in strict legislation to outlaw heavily polluting two-stroke engines, especially those over 125cc. It seems inevitable that eventually the pressure will be on, in the interest of cleaner air, not only to remove two-strokes from our roads but to convert to electric scooters only — with no exceptions.

GOING THE EXTRA MILE

Cesare Battaglini's Lambretta 150D may not be the prettiest of scooters but it probably has more stories to tell than any other. As a young man Battaglini dreamed of strange people, unexplored forests, wild mountains, never-ending deserts and a thousand other things that he thought he would never see, then decided to do something about it.

After a preliminary trip to Lapland he planned his great adventure — to discover the rest of the world. For transportation he chose a favourite Lambretta and had it specially prepared by Innocenti. Setting off in 1956, he traversed every inhabitable continent. Originally estimated at two years, this daunting expedition eventually took more than three years to complete and covered 160,000 kilometers — equivalent to circumnavigating the world four times.

Battaglini took the expression 'going the extra mile' to a new dimension by traversing Indochina, Indonesia, China, Australia, New Caledonia, New Zealand, Polynesia, North, South and Central America and on to Africa before returning to Italy. Along the way he took in the savannah of Pakistan complete with camel-riding nomads, the Sphinx and the Pyramids, the battlefield of El Alamein in Egypt, sacred dancers and floods in India, an African sorcerer, Moroccan rebels and even the State Capitol building in California.

Ferdinando Innocenti had provided welcome assistance by sending out spare parts and directing local dealers to help out and provide funding when necessary. In return Innocenti received valuable feedback on what needed to be improved on his doughty scooter. Sometimes Battaglini would take time out from his travels to teach the art of repairing Lambrettas, further spreading the word.

The little scooter designed for comparatively short-haul use had exceeded all expectations and blazed the Lambretta name across six continents. Achieving the seemingly impossible, Cesare Battaglini became a legendary figure who inspired many other scooter advocates to attempt similar feats.

CESARE BATTAGLINI'S MODIFIED LAMBRETTA 150D

GLOBAL REACH AND EFFECT

The motor scooter has found a home in every inhabitable continent in the world — regardless of ethnicity, creed or political ideals. Much of the credit for this success is due to Enrico Piaggio. His indefatigable efforts to promote his product included setting up service points and nurturing Vespa clubs in countries throughout the world.

Piaggio's production figures for 1946 were 2,484. The following year they were up to over 10,000. By 1950 output rose to above 60,000. Three years later 170,000 units rolled off the lines and production had begun in Germany, Britain, France, Spain and Belgium. Outlets in India and Brazil followed and before long the Vespa was produced in 13 countries and sold in 114 including Australia, South Africa, Iran and China. June 1956 saw total production reach the million mark with 10,000 service points established. And so the crusade rolled on, outselling motorcycles by that time.

Dozens of British, German and other manufacturers, having not

SCOOTER CLUBS AROUND THE WORLD

quite got it right, had fallen by the wayside. Meanwhile the Lambretta was beginning to enjoy some success. Following the trail blazed by Piaggio, Lambetta factories of one sort or another were set up in Italy, Spain, India, France, Germany, Argentina, Brazil, Congo, Colombia, Indonesia, Formosa, Pakistan and Turkey. Britain was notably not on the list but here Lambretta took advantage of the mess Piaggio had got into with Douglas and easily outsold the Vespa, importing as many as 100,000 in 1959 alone.

Motor scooter clubs proliferated in every continent with a great many originals still in existence today. Although Vespa can claim the lion's share, there is a significant Lambretta presence and many others for lesser-known makes. There is a veritable atlas of different club badges today that span the globe with hundreds

of clubs in Britain alone.

Scooter owners themselves helped to popularise the machines by embarking on incredible feats across the world even before Cesare Battaglini's epic three-year journey criss-crossing the globe. Originally conceived for relatively short-distance

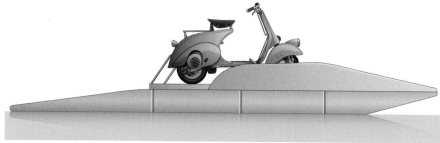

GEORGES MONNERET CROSSES THE ENGLISH CHANNEL WITH A VESPA 125 IN 1952

travel, the scooter looked beyond a trip to the seaside and set its sights on more adventurous journeys.

In 1952 Georges Monneret entered the Paris-London race and instead of waiting for the ferry he crossed the English Channel at the second attempt using a pontoon craft that was propeller-driven by his Vespa's rear wheel via a roller.

In 1954, Italian student Giorgio Ormoretti embarked on his own 77,000-mile trek aboard his Model D Lambretta that took him north of the Arctic Circle, through Europe and the Middle East then across Africa to arrive in Cape Town.

André Baldet chose to conquer Snowdon, the highest mountain in Wales, in 1955 with his 125cc Vespa ballasted with sand bags to prevent it tipping over backwards. In the Swiss Alps, Jean Stuper modified his Lambretta D by fitting a caterpillar track to the rear wheel and replaced the front wheel with a ski. This allowed him to get around the snow-covered slopes in almost all weather conditions.

Guy Montin had a different idea. After adapting his Lambro FD, in 1956, by building a plywood and canvas cabin on the back, he took his wife and two children on a journey from Sydney, Australia to Margate, England. The three-month journey covered 12,000 miles at a modest maximum speed of 25mph.

Such feats continued when Jeff Parker drove his Lambretta Model D to the top of Ben Nevis in five hours. Giancarlo Tironi, an Italian university student, reached the Arctic Circle on

a Vespa. The Argentine Carlos Velez crossed the Andes from Buenos Aires in Argentina to Santiago in Chile. Roberto Patrignani rode from Milan to Tokyo. Tommy Behan and Joan Short got their Vespa from London to Paris on just £1 of petrol. Australian Geoff Dean took his scooter on a round-the-world tour and Betty Warral decided to go a bit further than the supermarket and rode her Vespa from England to Australia and back.

Not to be outdone, Nigerian Olabis iAjala bought a Lambretta Li in England, circa 1960, and set off to circumnavigate the world. A freelance journalist, he met many world leaders along the way. These included the Soviet Union's Nikita Khrushchev, Egypt's President Nasser,

GIORGIO ORMORETTI ARRIVES IN CAPE TOWN IN 1954

Israeli Prime Minister Golda Meir, the Shah of Iran, Pandit Nehru in India, Prince Sihanouk of Cambodia and Chiang Kai-shek in Taiwan. Doubtless

his interviews paid for his petrol.

It seemed that, with a spare wheel and a couple of luggage racks, there was nowhere that was out of bounds for these little scooters. They exceeded the wildest expectations of Enrico Piaggio and Ferdinando Innocenti. When the first units rolled off the lines in northern Italy, neither could have imagined that they would be seen in the Arctic Circle or remote places like Tibet.

This adventurous tradition continued over the decades and into the present day. Giorgio Bettinelli made several trips that took him to places like Saigon, Alaska, Tierra del Fuego, Melbourne, Cape Town, Chile and Tasmania. In total he traversed six continents and clocked up 254,000km, which equates to about three-quarters

of the distance to the moon.

Markus aka Don Calvo started his great adventures in 2014 on his 1979 Vespa P200E, named 'Madalina', when it was already 35 years old. His touring around Europe was followed by setting an unofficial world record on a modern Scomadi TL125 scooter, riding 1,691km in 24 hours and passing through 10 countries. Scomadis apart, *La Vida Vespa* became a way of life for Markus, who made a big trip every year until he took up the Jules Verne-inspired challenge of 'Around The World In 80 Days'. Setting off on his trusted Vespa on 30 June 2018, he easily completed this daunting undertaking on 17 September — exactly 80 days later.

The scooter effect has reached far-off places, ranging from affluent

A CHEERFUL VESPA ADHERENT IN ZANZIBAR

countries to places like Uganda, one of the poorest of nations.

The island of Zanzibar is home to thousands of Vespas that are used for daily transportation and also by

the Simba Vespa Club Zanzibar. The Simba Apartment Hotel offers a 10% discount for Vespa drivers and can provide a scooter on arrival for touring the island's breathtaking landscapes.

The younger generation in Uganda prefer modern motorcycles and so the Vespa is regarded as a throwback to the past. The older generation of owners feel differently. They are proud of their iconic machines that were once seen as status symbols and form a tight-knit community who love their scooters as far as it is possible to love a machine. There is no great affection for needless chrome or fancy customised paintwork but they have an appreciation for their quality

and functional ability in keeping communities together. Nathan Mubiru owns a 54-year-old Vespa and believes it can serve at least 20 more years with care, attention and the availability of spare parts.

Seven thousand miles away there is a different perspective on the perennial motor scooter. Youth groups in Tokyo have embraced the idea of early Italian scooters and, emulating the originals, have created a Mod revival movement. Vespas and Lambrettas are sought-after and can expect to have an even more extended life in Japan, where teenagers have captured the style and attitude of the British Mods from the 1960s. On the other side of the world a similar thing is happening in Sweden.

TOKYO MOD REVIVALISTS
Photographer: Bruce Osborn

Creativity will not be denied and people will continue to use scooters as a means of expressing themselves. This can take very different forms. An older, more affluent group in Japan, who have the means to make their concepts achievable, have created a custom scene that is influenced by American lowrider cars. The basis for the creation shown on the next page is the Yamaha Majesty, a modern maxi scooter with a 400cc engine. A custom frame stretches the wheelbase and sets the motor further back with the rear wheel clear of the body. The lowrider look is made possible by fitting an air suspension system that can adjust the ride height. Adding a fabulous paint job with intricate detailing and LED under-lighting gives a unique and visually stunning result.

In Germany there are enough enthusiastic members of the Goggo Club to keep hundreds of their scooters active on the road, many in pristine condition. This kind of affection is repeated elsewhere.

YAMAHA MAJESTY LOWRIDER

The motor scooter's effect has reverberated around the world, influencing the culture and economic fortunes of many countries. Helping to regenerate the economies of Italy and Japan has since been followed by getting people and business moving in India, Thailand, China and many other countries in the Eastern Hemisphere. Together with the cultural aspect of giving people an identity, a new level of social freedom and communication in areas with little public transport, it has played a significant part within the infrastructure of countless nations. Between delivering babies and serving in the military, it has shown its versatility with every kind of small business.

With the phasing out of vehicles running on fossil fuels and the advent of electric replacements, most of this will continue. Yet it seems that the long-distance adventures of the earlier intrepid enthusiasts will become a thing of the past because of the short range of electric scooters and the problem of recharging in remote places.

Nearly all of the early scooter manufacturers are now defunct. Even Lambretta, which was reborn in India, ceased production in 1997. Piaggio survived and has now built more than 18 million vehicles in total but scooter manufacturing has shifted from the Western to the Eastern hemisphere. Now millions are produced in the East, predominantly in China and India. Many of these new products look much the same.

When it comes to diversity there is no

better example than the Extreme Vespa cult in Indonesia, where 85% of households own a scooter. The members are known as Rebel Riders and their passion is the Vespa. These scooters first appeared in the 1960s and by the 1970s were being manufactured in Jakarta. At the turn of the new millennium the scrapyards bulged with cast-off relics. The emergence of the Rebel Riders came after the repressive regime of President Soharto ended in 1998. The country then entered a period of new-found freedom and self-expression.

The Rebel Riders are numbered in their thousands and have little of what is known in the West as disposable income. Slick paintwork and chrome are not on the agenda. Neither is the speed of British machines. Surface rust

EXTREME VESPA WITH STRETCHED FRAME

and a few dents are of no consequence. The main factor is creativity — and the more extreme the better. Lack of funds is made up for by ingenuity and improvisation. This manifests itself in the form of miniature hot rods and tanks, extended vehicles, any number of extra wheels and stretched frames — there is no limit. One example is made from a hefty tree branch and has covered thousands of kilometres. This group has created a community that has become their way of life. Their adopted mantra 'My Vespa is your Vespa' means that in the event of a breakdown help is always at hand. Riding their largely unlicensed machines at night to avoid attention from the police, they visit many events across the islands each year, some attracting up to 50,000 spectators. Their devotion and camaraderie have set a unique standard.

TO INFINITY AND BEYOND?

Although the two-stroke engine is an endangered species, the scooter itself is reproducing in ever greater numbers. There is now a never-ending passing parade of new kids on the block. These are taking a different approach from early originals that first appeared in the post-war period.

The pinnacle of Lambretta design in the 1960s has so much charisma that modern manufacturers are still trying to recapture it. Scomadi is a British-based company that has created a new brand, manufactured in Thailand. The visual concept is clearly modelled on the Lambretta GP but things are a little different underneath. Motive power is provided by a four-stroke engine for better emissions and drive is provided by a CVT unit. Early limited editions of 250cc and 300cc have given way to the TL 125cc and the TL 200cc models.

Austrian design house KISKA is marketing its product under the brand of Lambretta. Named the V-Special, it is available in 50cc, 125cc and 169cc four-stroke engine sizes with CVT transmission. It is more or less the same engine unit as the SYM Fiddle twist-and-go scooter. Although clearly

2016 SCOMADI TL200 – BRITAIN

2017 KISKA LAMBRETTA V 125 FOUR-STROKE – AUSTRIA

influenced by the slim-style Lambrettas, it also adopts the stance of more modern machines and there are plans to develop an electric version.

The Chinese-made Neco Abruzzi is an unashamed clone of the Vespa but only in outward appearance. In reality it has a steel frame adorned by plastic bodywork to replicate the famous Wasp. It features a fuel-injected 125cc four-stroke, CVT drive, disc brakes front and rear, a digital dash and plug-in diagnostics. This scooter's use of modern technology with retro styling is well liked.

Piaggio itself is still exploring the possibilities. Moving away from the classic look that Neco has cloned, Piaggio beefed up the Vespa and gave it more rakish, angular lines with the 2008 introduction of the GTS 300 model. The engine also provides more muscle with a 300cc four-stroke pumping out 20+hp, which is pushed through a CVT drive to attain speeds of over 70mph. Digital instrumentation completes a modern redesign that is more reliable and easier to maintain.

The fact that four-strokes cause less pollution than two-strokes is not an

2017 NECO ABRUZZI WITH HONDA GY6 125 FOUR-STROKE – CHINA

2008 VESPA GTS SUPER 300 FOUR-STROKE – ITALY

97

environmental solution because the problem now is worse than ever due to the vastly greater numbers of scooters on the world's roads. Things reached a point in Shanghai when all petrol-powered scooters were eliminated by 2008 and gradually replaced by alternatives using Liquid Petroleum Gas (LPG). However, anyone thinking that this was a technological breakthrough would be very wide of the mark.

In Florida, way back in 1955, Ralph Carlton adapted his Cushman scooter

1955 RALPH CARLTON'S CUSHMAN SCOOTER ADAPTED TO RUN ON LPG – USA

2004 BENZHOU 125 LPG SCOOTER – CHINA

to run on LPG. By making some simple modifications and strapping an LPG tank to the front of the bike (safety standards were rather lenient in his day), he created an even more economical vehicle that was also 'eco-friendly'. Judging by the logo on the side, as pictured above, he was also promoting LPG sales.

The Benzhou Vehicle Industry Group began making LPG-powered scooters, like the one on this page, in 2004. Before long there were around 250,000 such vehicles on the road in Shanghai alone. This proved to be a false dawn. Gas leakage led to these types being branded a safety hazard and they were outlawed in 2014. Now all scooter owners are required to switch to electric.

Unsurprisingly electric technology is also nothing new. A patent appeared for an electric two-wheeler as early as 1897 and the first land speed record was set by an electric car. The Belgian company Socovel produced the first practicable electric scooter in 1936. The Socovel had a conventional lightweight frame carrying a large battery box containing three 12-volt batteries that powered a

1936 SOCOVEL ELECTRIC SCOOTER – BELGIUM

motor rated at 2.6hp. This vehicle's cruising speed of 16–20mph and range of 27 miles was limited because the batteries accounted for half of the scooter's 440lb weight. Even so, Socovel sold 1,000 units before production ceased and the initiative became forgotten.

Sixty years later in France, Peugeot produced its first electric scooter and introduced nickel-cadmium batteries in 1996. This was successful enough to lead to the launch of the e-Vivacity in 2011. A range of 37 miles at 25mph was not a quantum leap from the Socovel but development is now underway in this field all over the world.

2011 PEUGEOT E VIVACITY ELECTRIC SCOOTER – FRANCE

THE ELECTRIC DEVOLUTION

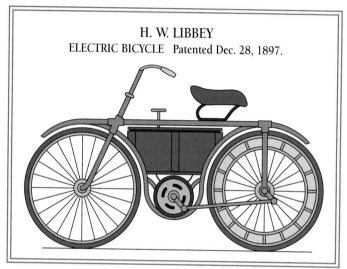

H. W. LIBBEY
ELECTRIC BICYCLE   Patented Dec. 28, 1897.

ONE OF THE EARLIEST RECORDED PATENTS

2020 HONDA PCX ELECTRIC

The arrival of electric vehicles is often seen as cutting-edge technology and of great benefit in keeping our planet green. But things are not always what they seem. Electric vehicles go back a long way, to 1897, when H.W. Libbey recorded a patent for an electric two-wheel vehicle. Although his idea never went into production, many electric cars did and by the 1900s they easily outsold those with internal combustion engines. Gradually the petrol-fuelled cars developed their potential and the electric cars found themselves handicapped with a short range, low speeds and heavy batteries that took hours to recharge. This has proved to be an enduring problem through a century's lack of development.

In 2020 the Honda PCX electric scooter did not show a quantum leap from 100 ago. Its looks may be influenced by speedy motorcycles but it has a range of only 25 miles and a top speed of just 37mph. One improvement, though, is that being much smaller than an electric car, it has a battery pack that has been designed to be swapped in seconds for a fully charged replacement. Provided that a replacement battery is readily available, this eliminates the charging time but still confines this scooter mostly to short-distance urban use. Epic journeys and high-speed cruising are not feasible. But this type of machine represents the future.

For centuries mechanical power was provided by eco-friendly windmills and water mills. When James Watt made his improvements to the steam engine during the latter part of the 18th century, it became capable of sustained usable power and lit the fuse for the industrial revolution. Britain's industrial centres soon sprouted forests of tall chimneys. Each one represented an individual steam engine fuelled by coal, which was also used for domestic heating. And so 'King' coal began to decorate every building with grimy soot and create dense, sulphurous fogs.

As the 20th century progressed, the numerous tall chimneys began to disappear as they were replaced by massive power stations burning coal, oil and gas, and creating ever more power and ever more pollution. This was repeated around the world. Whereas dense fogs had been shrugged off as a

SATANIC SCENE OF THE COAL-FIRED INDUSTRIAL REVOLUTION

TWENTIETH CENTURY POWER STATION

localised problem, the spectre of global pollution began to develop. This was worsened by the increasing number of fossil-fuelled vehicles on the road.

The industrial output of the world now demands ever more electrical energy to power the factories. Attempts to provide energy with reduced pollution are proving to be difficult. Coal and oil are still major contributors and alternatives present other problems.

Nuclear power stations are clean only to a degree because they have created thousands of tons of radioactive waste that remains a health hazard for many decades. No one knows what to do with it and no solution is in sight.

Hydro-electric power seems to be a viable answer because it is genuinely clean with no polluting side effects. There could be much more of it if its generation did not have to be confined to specific topographical sites. However, there can be other problems. The Three Gorges Dam in China is the biggest power station in the world producing 22.5 gigawatts — enough energy to power Switzerland. The downside is that 1.4 million people have been displaced and some view it as an ecological disaster. Wind-powered turbines produce clean energy but only run when wind speeds are suitable.

The world is now well aware of the consequences of increased pollution. The danger is staring us in the face.

Fig.5 shows the increase in pollution since 1900 (A); levels had increased by 50% by 1950 (B); at the turn of the century (C) they had risen by more than 200%. Fig.6 shows the increase in vehicle production since 1950. These two graphs, despite their different starting dates, show obvious correlation. The biggest culprits behind global pollution are the production of electricity followed by vehicle emissions.

Other graphs dealing with population increase, plastics production, contamination of the oceans by plastics, energy consumption, coal mining, crude oil production, industrial output, deforestation and many more all share the same inexorable upward progress. In principle it is almost a case of one graph fits all.

The answer, as any 10-year-old will tell us, is to reduce emissions. The problem is that the worst offenders depend on their economies to maintain the lifestyle to which they have become accustomed and fail to acknowledge that the piper must always be paid. The

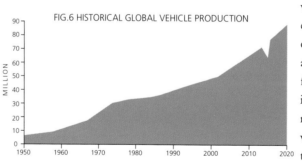

FIG.5 HISTORICAL GLOBAL POLLUTION LEVELS

FIG.6 HISTORICAL GLOBAL VEHICLE PRODUCTION

green alternatives to fossil fuels do not show enough promise. At the moment all these methods combined represent less than 10% of electricity output. Nuclear plants must find a way of safely disposing of their contaminated waste. To provide a complete alternative, hydro-electric power would have a serious impact on living space. Wind turbines would have to number in the millions to compete on a significant scale.

Faced with these seemingly insurmountable problems, we have turned our attention to reinventing the electric vehicles that were humming around a century ago. These have a great selling point in that they are emissions-free while in use, although the electricity to run them, of course, has to be generated and 85% of it is from fossil-fuelled power stations. There is also the energy involved in manufacturing them. These vehicles are more economical to run and may slow down the detrimental effect but even so the line on the graphs continue to rise.

China is leading the way with electric vehicles and has begun legislating fossil-fuelled motor scooters out of existence in favour of electric versions that already are said to number above 100 million. However, if energy is regarded as a commodity, the scrapping of earlier machines before their time means that all the energy invested in their manufacture is wasted. Manufacturing the new electric scooters requires yet more energy and to provide the electricity for them more coal-fired power stations — the dirtiest energy producers — are on the drawing board. Yet another problem is the increased use of plastic in manufacture instead of recyclable metal, plastics being derived from fossil-fuel sources. Nevertheless, here are a few examples of the future.

The NIU NGiGTS Pro, built in Changzhou, China is rated at around 45mph with a range of 60 miles and weighs 105kg. Its charge time is three and a half hours. Extras include a full-colour dashboard, app connectivity, USB port, electronic braking (EBS), anti-theft system, GPS tracking and cruise control.

The Lifan E3 is manufactured in Chongqing, China. Its top speed of 30mph and range of 45 miles are both less than the NIU NGiGTS Pro but so is the price. This is further reflected in the

NIU NGiGTS

LIFAN E3

103

SUPER SOCO CUx

TERRA MOTORS A4000i

longer charge time of six hours. Its low weight adds to its suitability for cost-effective, short-distance commuting.

Manufacturer claims for range and speed should be regarded with a certain amount of circumspection because they depend on different factors. For example, only a scooter with a lightweight driver on a straight, flat road with no oncoming wind will get optimum battery duration.

Like the Lifan E3, the Super Soco CUx, made in Shanghai, China, is designed for short journeys in 30mph city limits. In the lower weight bracket at 81kg, it claims a range of 40 miles at a modest 28mph but with the longer charge time of six to seven hours. Like most electric scooters, it features disc brakes front and rear. Extras include an LCD screen, keyless technology with a motion-activated alarm, EBS assistant and app integration.

Terra Motors in Tokyo, Japan arranged a partnership with the Jahanro Industrial Co. to sell its A4000i electric scooter in Iran. The capital Tehran is one of the most polluted cities in the world and is clogged with fossil-fuelled two-wheelers. These

VESPA ELETTRICA

SUZUKI BURGMAN

machines are all to be outlawed and replaced with new electric types. The A4000i has a speed of 40mph and a range of 40 miles. Charging time is four and a half hours and its weight is 118kg. Being cheaper to run, it has been of benefit to many who are on a low level of subsistence.

Vespa brought its rich history full circle in 2016 with the introduction of its own electric scooter. Maintaining the distinctive Wasp styling, the Elettrica was unveiled. Costing double the price of the economy Chinese versions, it offered a 60-mile range, 35mph and a charging time of four hours. It was also heavier at 130kg. Seventy years earlier, the first Vespa 90 offered 37mph and 118 miles per gallon. The Elettrica is undoubtedly technically superior and creates less pollution but, in the great scheme of things, by exactly how much is debatable.

The next breakthrough is the hydrogen scooter. The key to this is the fuel cell, as used in the space shuttle, to provide electricity, giving it the aura of space-age technology. Suzuki has a scooter in the development stage called the Burgman with a claimed range of

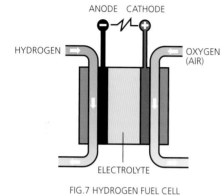

ANODE CATHODE

HYDROGEN ⇨

⇦ OXYGEN (AIR)

ELECTROLYTE

FIG.7 HYDROGEN FUEL CELL

90 miles and a speed of 43mph.

The principle of the fuel cell was conceived by Sir William Grove in 1839 when he mixed hydrogen and oxygen in the presence of an electrolyte to produce electricity and water. The amount of current generated was negligible and it was not until 1959 that Francis T. Bacon made enough improvements for the fuel cell to reveal its potential as a practical proposition.

This system is like all electric scooters in that the drive is by an electric motor. The current is provided by a fuel cell, which, unlike a battery, will not run flat but will go on producing a charge as long as hydrogen is present. The fuel cell (Fig.7) consists of an anode and a cathode with an electrolyte in between. When hydrogen is channelled past the anode and oxygen, in the form of air, is channelled past the cathode, an electric current is created. Each fuel cell contains multiple individual cells and the only emission is water.

Hydrogen is the most plentiful element on our planet, so is the pollution problem solved? Unfortunately, we can never select the one result we want to the exclusion of all others. At present over 90% of commercial hydrogen derives from fossil fuels. A small amount is created through electrolysis, which itself requires generated electricity in large amounts.

Another problem is filling stations and storage. Compressing hydrogen to a liquid would reduce container size and enhance the range of vehicles but this involves pressures of up to 10,000 pounds per square inch and again involves a lot of energy.

It becomes obvious that we cannot get something for nothing and must look to the least damaging solutions.

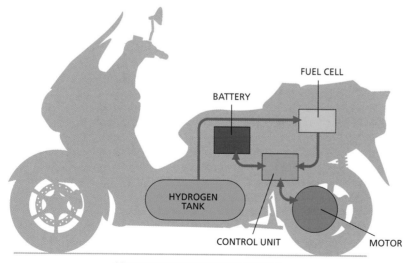

FUEL CELL

BATTERY

HYDROGEN TANK

CONTROL UNIT

MOTOR

SCHEMATIC OF HYDROGEN CELL SCOOTER

A COKE AND A BASEBALL HAT

Great Britain was known as the workshop of the world until America took over as the biggest exporter and was tagged the land of opportunity. Countries in the eastern hemisphere have looked to the west and aspired to the American Dream in which everyone seemingly enjoyed an affluent lifestyle with a car, fridge and TV. The allure of a better lifestyle has manifested itself in American totems. Coca-Cola and baseball caps are sold in almost every country in the world regardless of political ideology, religious affiliation or ethnicity.

The way that most Far Eastern countries are pursuing the dream is to expand their industrial economies. By harnessing mass production with exploited labour, they are able to produce goods that are cheaper than is possible in the West.

China is now the globe's industrial giant and its products are in great demand in the West. Paradoxically, this has brought criticism because of the pollution created: China is now a much greater polluter than America, which is the second biggest culprit with India third in line (Fig.8). Yet if the amount of pollution per person is the criterion, a very different picture emerges

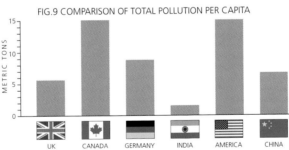

FIG.8 COMPARISON OF TOTAL POLLUTION PER COUNTRY

FIG.9 COMPARISON OF TOTAL POLLUTION PER CAPITA

(Fig.9). Canada and America are the most wasteful and China's figures are better than Germany's. Like many a bad football team losing a match, the countries of the world have resorted to arguing among themselves.

Industry's demand for electricity is more than ever before. Piaggio took 13 years to reach a total production figure of two million. Now there are that many scooters produced globally each month. The East is awash with millions of them. China is leading the way with electric versions and producing them in vast numbers. Electric vehicles are better than fossil-fuel burners but the fact is that we are worse off than ever because the dirty two-strokes of the 1960s were far less numerous.

Converting to electric vehicles is not going to reduce pollution. The human race occupies just one period in the eons of time: we are simply living in the 'now', a sort of dreamland where much is said but the problems facing humanity keep getting worse.

Our wounded planet will no doubt recover given the chance. In the meantime, since it is more economical for one or two people to get from A to B on a scooter than in a car, maybe the electric motor scooter can help eke out our finite reserves for a while longer.

INDEX

Romolo Ferri's 1951 record of 124.89mph is as yet unbeaten by any 125cc Lambretta.

Romolo Ferri lines up for his 1951 record attempt with the Innocenti Lambretta streamliner.